# INTERNATIONAL MARIJUANA

## 2019 Edition

# The No B.S. Guide to Investing in Weed Stocks Globally

Profit from the legalization of Cannabis in
Canada, Australia, Israel, Europe, U.S. and More

Written by Peter Hatcher, PFA

# Table of Contents

# Introduction

Wouldn't it have been nice to own shares of Anheuser-Busch in the 1930's just after prohibition was repealed? Even since 1997, its share price has increased a full 1000% to well over $100 per share. That doesn't even consider its stock splits. This global company now has a market share of nearly 50% in the U.S. alone.

Well now there's an opportunity to own the Anheuser-Busch of the future.

As most people know, millions of investors are already reaping stock market profits in a fast-emerging industry still at ground zero-- the Cannabis industry. *Newsmax* quoted an analyst saying that the "Medical Marijuana industry is projected to Top $40 billion dollars by 2020" in the U.S.

Unfortunately, in the United States, marijuana is still classified as a "Schedule 1" drug on par with heroin and LSD. Consequently, expansion for companies will be difficult. Therefore, the next Anheuser-Busch will likely not be in the U.S. It will be abroad!

The U.S. is one of at least 20 countries on the path to country-wide legalization. In fact, there are countries like Canada and Luxembourg that just legalized Marijuana in the last 12 months and their stocks are already exploding. Right this instant, publicly traded companies in these countries are tracking to be the next Anheuser-Busch. For all these reasons, millions of investors are turning to foreign companies all around the world.

For instance, a report from the University of Sydney stated the initial demand for medical cannabis in Australia could be worth more than $100 M a year. This is expected to expand to $300 M a year should recreational cannabis become legal as well. In addition, at the time of this writing, marijuana stocks have dominated the trading on Canada's TSX Venture index, averaging around 10 per cent of the volume on the total exchange!

Did you know you can buy shares of these companies too, regardless of physical location and citizenship? You don't have to be an insider. This book will teach you how!

The following pages are a direct, no-nonsense guide to making easy profit by investing in these global companies. Some of what you'll learn includes:

-A guide on how to choose an online brokerage firm that allows you to buy international stocks cheaply.

-20 countries that just legalized cannabis or are legalizing soon.

-The 18 best, safest, fastest growing marijuana related companies trading on public exchanges around the world. Based on their management, partnerships, contracts and spreadsheets, these companies are currently competing for global market share.

-Planned Marijuana-related IPOs of 2019. These private companies of today may be the hot weed stocks of tomorrow.

-A guide on how to do further research on the selected companies in this book and future companies that have yet to enter the market.

-Trading strategy tips including position trading, swing trading, entry and exit points, margin trading and more.

-Online resources and more!

Around the world, cannabis is becoming as common as getting prescription medicine. In the next few years, it may become as common as a bottle of wine. Therefore, make sure you study the material in this book. Get your ticket to the "International Green Rush" before it's too late!

# Getting Started

Before we get into the nitty gritty, let me first say this book already assumes you have experience as a stock trader. Experienced stock traders understand there is no such thing as winning trades 100% of the time. It cannot be done. And this is especially true when investing in stocks growing within an industry just now becoming legal.

Why? Outside of the top 10 marijuana stocks mentioned in this book, many of these stocks are thinly traded. Therefore, they can be quite volatile.

However, the good news is volatility can be extremely profitable-- especially within an emerging industry such as this one. And with an industry such as this one, if you are patient and you properly diversify your capital within several of the different stocks mentioned later, the chances of seeing considerable returns is definitely in your favor. Companies that can successfully make the leap from penny to a blue-chip stock are rare, but savvy investors have already managed to rake in gains of over 1,000% within a few years with stocks like Canadian Marijuana producer, Aurora Cannabis.

If you're looking for modest returns like 3%, it would be better for you to buy an ETF that tracks the S&P 500. However, at the time of this writing, you're better off throwing your cash out the window. With the recent downturn, most of the overvalued stocks included in the index will continue to tumble. Many experts believe these stocks have not reached the bottom, due to the instability created by the trade war with China, political turmoil at the White House, growing interest rates by the Fed, and figures showing the economy is generally slowing down. If you want explosive returns, the strategy should be to buy stocks with enormous potential and upside.

At the time of this writing, many marijuana stocks are still penny stocks. This is not necessarily because the companies are terribly run (although some may be), but because the cannabis industry is in its infancy-- and just now becoming legal. The friction between federal illegality and the state legality means uncharted waters. Until this year, the Nasdaq and the New York Stock Exchange have generally wanted no part of this until the friction ends. Therefore, to get access to capital, these companies have used reverse mergers and other mechanisms to end up being publicly traded on over-the-counter exchanges.

OTC exchanges are not taken as seriously as the bigger exchanges. While exchanges like NYSE are tough on quality, OTC generally allows for a greater degree of latitude for the companies that trade on them. As a result, solid marijuana companies like Terra Tech Corp. (TRTC) and mCig Inc. (MCIG) probably shouldn't be on the OTC exchanges. They got there because entrepreneurs thought it was the only way they could get access to capital. After all, with federal illegality still a reality, even a bank loan is nearly impossible.

This is also true in other countries with their own version of OTC exchanges. However, once the U.S. and other countries legalize medical and recreational pot across the board and real earnings start pouring in, it can mean double, triple, or even 10x the profit for these stocks within a few years.

Don't forget, since these stocks are often thinly traded, diversification and risk management are key. For those of you not as equipped with experience in stock trading, this book also contains time-tested stock trading tips and guidelines in subsequent chapters for your quick and easy reference. These useful tips are not at all revolutionary. However, they are often missed as traders let their emotions rule their decisions.

# Cannabis 101

## Overview

Before plunging head first into marijuana stocks, it is prudent to understand the ins and outs of the industry as well as the plant itself. Each of these companies have products and services related to different aspects of cannabis. While one company may be a producer that grows and sells cannabis, another company may function by leasing the real estate the producer operates on. To make wise investment choices, an investor should know everything there is to know about cannabis. If you are already well-versed, by all means skip to whatever chapter you are ready for.

## Cannabis and Cannabinoids

Taken and prepared from the cannabis plant, cannabis is also referred to as 'marijuana' or 'weed'. The most well-known psychoactive part of cannabis, known to make people feel "stoned", is tetrahydrocannabinol (THC); one of 65 other cannabinoids. Cannabinoids are any of a group of closely related compounds found in cannabis that include cannabidiol (CBD).

As more scientific research is conducted involving cannabis and its ability to be used as a medicine, interest in CBD has grown exponentially. CBD does not make people feel "stoned" and actually counters some of the effects of THC. After decades of only high-THC marijuana being available, CBD-rich strains are now being grown for patients. CBD has been featured on numerous forms of media and publications showing how well it works in treating people. It is what ultimately led Mexico to pass recent legislation allowing marijuana for their patients who suffer from severe epilepsy.

Cannabis is intended for use as a drug or medicine in various forms, including smoking, food, through an inhaler, vaporization, etc. Whether it's for medicinal purposes or not, Cannabis users feel its effects within minutes when smoked, but longer when eaten. Included among these effects are a heightened mood, an altered change in perception and an increase in appetite. Short term side effects may include short-term memory issues, cottonmouth, impaired motor skills and feelings of paranoia. (Leafly.com)

# Various forms of Consumption

Cannabis is consumed in the following ways:

**1. Smoking**, which usually involves burning the cannabinoids and then inhaling vaporized cannabinoids through a small pipes or bong.

**2. Tea**, typically in which a mixture of cannabis is infused with fat (e.g., coconut oil, cream or butter) combined with tea leaves and water to make a chai or latte-type drink. You can even consider dissolving cannabutter into a cup of tea or coffee. These drinks have little to no psychoactive effects.

**3. Edibles**, in which cannabis or cannabis oils are infused into baked food items such as brownies and cookies. Because of the slow, tedious digestive process, edibles take much longer to kick in. However, they can have more intense psychoactive effects.

**4. Vaporizer**, a device used to heat up marijuana buds (around 390-something degrees F) to the point where the material (including the THC, Cbd/cbn, etc.) evaporates into a vapor form. Typically, the vapor is drawn in slower and held for longer than smoke, somewhere between 15-30 seconds. Its chemical compounds vaporize at a much lower, less harmful temperature. The taste of vaporized cannabis is often preferred to that of combusted flower. In addition, the vapor is much easier on the lungs.

**5. Ingestible Oils,** basically any cannabis concentrate that is taken orally. They can induce delayed, yet powerful effects much like edibles. They mostly come in capsules to be consumed with food and a drink.

**6. Topicals,** in which lotions and balms are infused with a mixture of cannabis. Thereafter, they can be applied directly to the skin for localized relief of pain or inflammation without psychoactive effects.

# Varieties

According to the United Nations Office on Drugs and Crime (UNODC), "the amount of THC present in a cannabis sample is generally used as a measure of cannabis potency." The three main forms of cannabis products are the flower, resin (hashish), and oil (hash oil).

## 1. Marijuana

Marijuana consists of the dried flower buds and leaves of the female Cannabis plant. This is the most popular form of consumption, containing 3% to 20% THC, with reports of up-to 33% THC.

## 2. Kief

Those small, sticky crystals that cover cannabis flower buds. Kief is the powder, rich in trichomes, which can accumulate in containers or be sifted from the leaves and flowers of cannabis plants. Trichomes keep away hungry animals by producing disorientation. Kief can either be consumed in powder form or compressed to produce cakes of hashish.

## 3. Hashish

Hashish is a concentrated resin cake or ball produced from compressed kief. It may also be produced by scraping the resin from the surface of the cannabis plant and rolling it into a ball. It can be consumed orally, smoked or vaporized.

## 4. Tincture

A solution of alcohol containing cannabinoids extracted from the cannabis plant. It is often referred to as "green dragon". The tincture is typically made by soaking the dried flower buds in ethanol and evaporating the solvent. The THC and other cannabinoids dissolve into the alcohol. The tincture is ordinarily consumed orally, but may also be applied to the skin.

## 5. Hash oil

It's the extracted oil from the Cannabis plant by solvent extraction, formed into a hardened or viscous mass. To make the oil, you grind up the pot, flush it with the solvent, then heat it and pressurize it to release the oil. The end product can have a consistency that ranges from that of olive oil to a hard and brittle toothpaste. Hash oil can be the most potent of the main cannabis products because of its high level of THC. The drug can be smoked or vaporized directly, or used to make edible products or balms.

## 6. Infusions

There are many varieties of cannabis infusions. The plant material is mixed with the solvent (such as dairy butter, cooking oil, ointments, etc) and then pressed and filtered to express the oils of the plant into the solvent. Cannabis is being infused in numerous products these days such as teas, cooking oils, massage oils, ointments and of course various edibles. More than ever, the list of products continues to grow.

# The Cannabis Strains: Sativa vs. Indica

Indica and Sativa are the two major types of cannabis plants. They can be mixed together to create hybrid strains. Each strain has its own range of effects on the body and mind, resulting in a wide range of medicinal benefits. Indica strains tend to be more psychoactive. They are physically sedating, perfect for relaxing before going to bed or watching a movie. With Sativa, a well-being, cerebral uplifting and ease is often associated. This makes them ideal for social gatherings and creative projects. (Leafly.com)

A patient suffering from fatigue or depression may use Sativa during the day. A different patient being treated for inflammation or insomnia, will likely choose an Indica strain at night. Most Indica varieties come from central Asia and the Indian subcontinent, while Sativa generally originates in the equatorial regions, such as Thailand and Mexico.

Visit the Marijuana Strain Explorer at Leafly.com, to see a list of the most popular versions of these cannabis strains. These include everything from girl scout cookies, Bubba Kush, Pineapple Express, Amnesia Haze and more.

# Choosing an International Online Brokerage

Smoking weed may be a pastime for some; but strides in medical marijuana research for countless diseases are causing FDA approvals to increase yearly. As the legalization of cannabinoids, THC, CBD and marijuana becomes more of a reality, millions of retail investors will continue to pour their money into the marijuana market. Short of starting your own company, it is likely better to invest in the stocks of viable cannabis related companies to get a piece of the billion dollar pie. The first step is selecting a brokerage firm in which you can trade international stocks cheaply.

Technology is making investing in stocks overseas cheaper and easier than ever before. Fortunately for us, we no longer have to leave our international stocks in the costly hands of institutional managers.

There are different ways to trade foreign stocks:

## American Depositary Receipt (ADR)

Introduced to the financial markets in 1927, an American depositary receipt (ADR) is a stock that trades in the U.S. but represents a specified number of shares in a foreign company. Issued by banks and brokers, ADRs are bought and sold on American public exchanges just like regular stocks. FInancial institutions price an ADR high enough to show substantial value, yet low enough to make it affordable for individual investors.

There are three different types of ADR issues. The most basic type of ADR represents foreign companies that don't qualify or don't wish to have their ADR listed on an exchange. They are found on the over-the-counter market and are an easy and inexpensive way to gauge interest for its securities in North America. Since they trade thinly, most international cannabis stocks found on U.S. exchanges will fall in this category.

## Non-ADR Stocks

To get your hands on a Non-ADR foreign stock or ORDs (ordinary shares), you have to have a broker that can convert dollars into a foreign currency. In addition, sometimes you have to pay another small fee to cover brokerage costs on a foreign exchange. The ordinary shares of foreign-based companies are not always officially listed on U.S. market exchanges. However, you can trade ORD stocks or trade funds that invest in ORD stocks through most of the brokers listed below.

# Top 4 Brokerage Firms for International Trading

Many online brokers, like Ally.com do not offer either ADR or Non-ADR securities for trading on their platforms. The best way to trade these stocks are through foreign-trading services offered by quality online firms like International Brokers, Fidelity Investments, Charles Schwab & Co and a few others. Determining which of these brokers has the better deal for you depends on how large is the amount of capital you will be trading with, the size of your transactions and how often you will be trading.

Furthermore, each of these brokers offer trading on margin. The amount of money you can borrow on margin toward the purchase of stocks is typically limited to 50 percent of the value of marginable securities in your account. However, it is prudent to borrow less to lower your risk. Once you borrow on margin, you are required to maintain a certain amount of value in your account, depending on the diversity of the securities you possess. Typically, the equity maintenance requirement is at least 30% of the total account value. Brokers calculate your buying power and cash available for withdrawal.

## 1. Interactive Brokers LLC.

Due to its transparency and its low costs, this broker is a top pick for professional traders. Lower commissions, no ticket charges; no minimums; no software, platform, or reporting fees; and extremely low financing rates.

## Trade Execution

IB offers great, quick execution of trades. Most brokers trade against your orders or sell them to others to execute who will trade against them. The resulting poor execution can result in costs higher than the commission you pay. IB continuously searches and reroutes to the best available prices for stocks and options. (interactivebrokers.com)

## Stock Yield Enhancement

There's even a way to safely make extra income through their Stock Yield Enhancement Program. The program lets them borrow shares in exchange for cash collateral, and then lends the shares to traders who are willing to pay a fee to borrow them. You will be paid a loan fee each day that your stock is on loan.

## Foreign Stocks

Most importantly, IB offers ADR stocks and non-ADR stocks. You can literally trade on over 100 market centers in 24 countries. You'll have direct market access to stocks, options, futures, forex, bonds, ETFs and CFDs from a single universal account. You can fund your account in multiple currencies and trade assets denominated in multiple currencies from a single account.

## Fees

Interactive Brokers differs from many other online brokerages by offering a trading fee structure based on the number of shares traded. Other brokerages, like the ones mentioned later in this chapter, have a flat fee. Interactive Brokers charges $0.0050 per share traded. That's great if you are buying less than a 1,000 shares. For instance, for a transaction of 250 shares, IB will only charge $1.25! However, if you plan on trading at a high volume, it may be better to go with a flat fee brokerage.

## Margin Rates

If you're looking to trade on margin, you will love the rates IB offers. They are extremely low. The maximum margin rate is the benchmark rate plus 1.5%. This blended rate is based on account balance. Larger cash balances receive increasingly better rates. For balances of $100,000 or less, the margin rate is currently only 2.16%! It only gets lower from there.

## Minimums

Interactive Brokers is able to maintain such low rates and fees because it requires a minimum of $10,000 to open an account with them. They make their money through the volume of activity of each customer. For those of you who do not have the funds for such a deposit, this may be a deal breaker. However, if you do have the funds, you'll save big on costs in the long run. To maintain the account thereafter, you must maintain at least $2,000 or non-USD equivalent in your account. Otherwise, fees may be collected.

For more current information, visit their website: interactivebrokers.com

## 2. Fidelity Investments

Fidelity is another great broker for trading foreign stocks. It is especially great for traders who want to keep a portion of their capital parked in a specific foreign currency for several years. You will pay the conversion rate, but low brokerage commissions.

For instance, after Fidelity turns your currency into Euros, you'll be able to do online trades in market exchanges of France, Germany, Belgium, etc. As with Interactive Brokers, all dividends received by you would remain in euros and your Fidelity account would show separate U.S. dollar and foreign currency credit balances.

**Fees**

In response to the growing competition, Fidelity lowered its commissions in February 2017, dropping from $7.95 per trade to $4.95. While not as low as IB, that's actually near the bottom among quality online brokers, especially considering the level of excellence the company's customer service provides.

**Margin Rates**

Fidelity offers relatively low margin rates. Like IB, the margin rate you pay depends on your outstanding margin balance. The higher your balance, the lower the margin rate you are charged. For balances between $0-$24,999, the margin rate is Base + 1.50%-- which at the time of this writing, translates to an effective rate of 8.325%. With balances of $25,000-$49,999, the effective rate is 7.825%. Between $50,000-$99,999, the rate is 6.875% and so on.

## Minimums

At the time of this writing, Fidelity has a minimum investment of $2,500 for brokerage accounts. that's fairly high compared with other online brokers. For IRA accounts, the minimum is $0. If you want to invest in mutual funds, most Fidelity and non-Fidelity funds carry a $2,500 minimum as well.

For more information (like current rates and fees), visit their website: www.fidelity.com.

## 3. Charles Schwab & Co.

Charles Schwab offers plenty of trading and educational features that many newbies will find useful. Schwab has extensive research tools at your fingertips and 24/7 customer service. Furthermore, customers who already possess a Schwab bank account or an OptionsXpress account can access all accounts through a single log-in.

### Fees

Like Interactive Brokers and Fidelity, Charles Schwab is ahead of most of its competitors with a $4.95 flat-rate for stock trades. The same goes for option trades, which run at $4.95, plus $.65 per contract. Investors trading ETFs will also enjoy Schwab as the leading broker in its offering of 229 commission-free ETFs. Interestingly, Schwab offers to refund fees or commission if for any reason you're not completely satisfied.

For foreign stocks, you pay a single fee covering both its brokerage commission and the currency conversion. However, there is an additional fee for the overseas broker. Schwab's fee is 0.5%, with a $100 minimum on trades smaller than $20,000. The overseas fee ranges from 0.4% to 1.2%.

## Margin Rates

Schwab's low margin rates are comparable to Fidelity. For balances between $0-$24,999, the current margin rate is 8.50%. With balances of $25,000-$49,999, the effective rate is 8.00%. Between $50,000-$99,999, the rate is 7.00% and so on. To begin borrowing at Schwab, you must have at least $5,000 in cash or marginable securities in your account.

## Minimums

To open an account with Schwab, the minimum deposit is $1,000. This minimum is waived if you set up an automatic monthly transfer of $100 through direct deposit or Schwab MoneyLink® or open a Schwab Bank High Yield Investor Checking® account linked to your brokerage account.

For more information (like current rates and fees), visit their website: www.schwab.com.

# 4. Scottrade, Inc.

At mostly only $7 per trade, Scottrade also offers access to foreign stocks from over 20 countries. Like the brokers mentioned earlier, Scottrade provides customers the ability to trade international equities alongside domestic equities via one central account.

## Foreign Stocks

Scottrade provides customers with advanced research and trading tools to help you manage investments intelligently and on your own terms.

Scottrade offers ADRs for companies in over 20 countries throughout Europe, Africa, South America, and Asia Pacific. Through an online trading account, you can use the stock screener to get online quotes and explore ADR stocks or ORDs that you can use to expand your portfolio's investments internationally. In addition, you can start your research online with news, charts and stock information for many international stocks, available free of charge with your Scottrade account.

## Fees

For customers at Scottrade, most array of products and services to help meet financial goals, are provided at no cost. Their trading fees and commissions are intentionally straightforward and clear. Lastly, they don't charge clients fees for account maintenance or inactivity. At the time of this writing, an online trade is only $7. If broker assisted, the fee is $32.

## Margin Rates

During the time your loan is outstanding, Scottrade charges interest daily based on the amount of funds you borrow. Keeping a higher debit balance in your account generally makes you eligible for lower interest rates. For instance, at the time of this writing, a loan balance under $9,999.99 results in an interest rate of 8.25% (Base Rate + 1.25%). Between $10,000 and $24,999.99, the interest rate is 8%.

An initial deposit of $2,000 is required to request margin privileges. Once a loan is extended, you're required to keep a minimum equity level, called the maintenance requirement, in your account if you're trading on margin or using margin loan privileges.

## Trade Execution

Scottrade regularly reviews and assesses market center performance to optimize trade speed and strongly compete against industry averages, helping to ensure orders are executed quickly and efficiently. At the time of this writing, their trade execution speed was 0.10 seconds. This number represents a 6-month rolling average for market orders (100-1999 Shares) in S&P 500 securities.

For more information (like current rates and fees), visit their website: www.scottrade.com/

# In Conclusion

For most investors, the strategy is to skip ORD shares. Buy ADRs only and to be patient with the ones that don't trade heavily. Yes, there are fees that can come with acquiring ADRs, but they are small (one to three cents a share annually). In fact, they are often picked up by the issuing company anyway.

Lastly, familiarize yourself with the technical aspects of your broker's trading platform by practicing through a demo account. Each broker has one. Practicing through a demo account is particularly important as this is the same platform you'll be using when you fund your account with real money. It will help you to master the mechanics of entering and exiting trades, not to mention avoid the many mistakes you might make otherwise.

# 20 Countries Legalizing Cannabis

## Overview

The legality of cannabis for general or recreational use varies from country to country. Due to an agreement about Indian hemp, also known as hashish, in the International Opium Convention (1925), possession of cannabis is still illegal in most countries. Currently, Canada (recently in 2018) and Uruguay are the only nations that have completely legalized cannabis for both recreational and medical use.

Recently in the last several years, there's been a wave of optimism as many first world countries have either decriminalized marijuana use, or in some-- like Germany and Australia, full legalization is on its way. There are currently 29 countries that recognize medical marijuana, but only two (Canada and the Netherlands) currently export beyond their borders.

Because legalization is such a new issue, many countries are looking to the United States to see how legalization is working out in states like California, Colorado, Nevada and Washington. So far, it has been a success. Some of the social and economic benefits include tax revenue increases and decreases in drug-related crime. Countries that have either decriminalized or legalized cannabis have seen positive results across the board, including lower traffic fatalities and opioid abuse, and even nerve cell protection.

In fact, few people know that the US government owns the original patent on Cannabinoids (Cannabis extracts) and lists them as "Neural Protectants" meaning they protect and repair nerves in the brain and body. (worldhealth.net)

# The Countries

The last 12 months have been absolutely stellar for the legal marijuana industry. The global market has nudged its way further into the hearts of culture and finance. California became the largest United States market, while Utah, Michigan, Vermont, Missouri and Oklahoma joined the party as well. Canada has now fully legalized pot, with both medicinal and recreational marijuana markets underway. And Mexico's Supreme Court is setting up the country to come on board as well.

Below is a list of some of the countries in which the legalization of cannabis is coming soon. With cannabis being such a burgeoning industry, the sooner you start your investments, the sooner you can ride the wave to enormous profits. However, countries that have had legal cannabis use for many years have been left out, because investment opportunities don't have as much upside. This includes Uruguay, Costa Rica, Netherlands and Spain.

# 1. United States

After his inauguration, it didn't take very long for the Trump Administration to kill the growing buzz surrounding weed legalization. In fact, it wasn't too long ago that Attorney General Jeff Sessions rescinded a policy that shielded state-licensed medical marijuana operators from federal drug prosecutions.

However, these policy makers couldn't stop the train.

Here is a list of just some of the highlights of 2018:

- January 1, One of the biggest economies in the world, California has its new marijuana law taking effect, allowing recreational marijuana use to anyone, as long as they meet age requirements.

- January 22, Vermont's Legislature legalizes recreational marijuana. This marks the first time a state legislature, rather than voters, approved this type of law.

- June 25, Seeing the need to treat two rare forms of epilepsy found in young children, U.S. health regulators approve Epidiolex, a drug derived from marijuana. The drug was created by GW Pharmaceuticals (NASDAQ: GWPH).

- June 28, Conservative Oklahoma becomes the 30th state to legalize medical marijuana use. This shows marijuana is increasingly becoming a bipartisan issue.

- July 19, Tilray Inc. (NASDAQ: TLRY) becomes the first marijuana company to complete an IPO on the Nasdaq exchange-- a major U.S. Stock Exchange, raising $153 million in its first days of trading.

- August 15, Constellation Brands Inc, the parent company of many alcoholic drinks including Corona invests $4 billion into Canopy Growth Corporation (NYSE: CGC). Other colossal brands like Coca Cola have also expressed interest in joining the marijuana revolution.

- November 7, Election day brings great news for the industry as Michigan becomes the 10th overall state to legalize recreational marijuana use, while Missouri and Utah amazingly approve medical marijuana.

- December 7th, Altra, a United States cigarette maker invests $2.4 billion into Cronos Group (NASDAQ: CRON), another publicly traded Canadian marijuana producer—a 45% stake.

**Federal Legalization**

However, medical and recreation use is still illegal on a federal level. Cannabis is still considered a Schedule 1 drug, meaning that the U.S. Drug Enforcement

Administration sees no medicinal properties in the substance and classifies it as highly addictive on par with LSD. Therefore, marijuana companies cannot even open a checking account or obtain a line of credit with banks because they're selling a federally illegal substance. If a bank did open an account or a line of credit for a company selling marijuana-related products, it could be construed as money laundering and expose them to substantial fines. In addition, "Marijuana businesses are severely hampered by U.S. Tax Code 280E, which disallows businesses that sell a federal illicit substance from taking normal business deductions." (The Motley Fool)

While the Obama administration decided not to interfere with state regulation, this current Trump administration, led by a very conservative house (until January) and senate, have not been as hands-off. However, while the Department of Justice can take legal action and enforce the federal Controlled Substances Act, if a state decides it does not want to use its courts and police to arrest and punish marijuana users, there is little the federal government can do to change that without using considerable resources.

**Hemp Officially Legalized**

On December 20th 2018, the White House and Congress legalized hemp with a broad farm bill, first introduced earlier this year. This farm bill, which mostly deals with agriculture subsidies and food assistance programs, will reclassify hemp as an agricultural crop.

While the move is essentially outright legalization, strict regulations still apply:

"Although hemp will no longer be in the jurisdiction of the Department of Justice, prospective growers will have to submit cultivation plans to the U.S. Department of Agriculture (USDA), either through the state government or the USDA itself. Cannabis plants must contain less than 0.3 percent THC in order to be classified as hemp." (marijuanamoment.net)

In addition, John Hudak of the Brookings Institute said, "It is true that section 12619 of the Farm Bill removes hemp-derived products from its Schedule I status under the Controlled Substances Act, but the legislation does not legalize CBD generally. As I have noted elsewhere on this blog CBD generally remains a Schedule I substance under federal law… The Farm Bill ensures that any cannabinoid—a set of chemical compounds found in the cannabis plant—that is derived from hemp will be legal, *if and only if* that hemp is produced in a manner consistent with the Farm Bill, associated federal regulations, association state regulations, and by a licensed grower. All other cannabinoids, produced in any other setting, remain a Schedule I substance under federal law and are thus illegal. (The one exception is pharmaceutical-grade CBD products that have been approved by FDA, which currently includes one drug: GW Pharmaceutical's Epidiolex.)" (marijuanamoment.net)

Hemp is derived from the cannabis plant, but it doesn't get you high like its cousin, Marijuana. Instead, it's typically used for its fiber to make all kinds of products, including food, paper, clothes and so much more.

## Mostly Penny Stocks

Many marijuana stocks in the U.S., like Terra Tech Corp. and mCig Inc., are penny stocks that are thinly traded over the counter rather than on one of the major exchanges. Many of these penny stocks are great companies. However, they cannot grow as fast when they can't even take out a bank loan.

If low risk is a priority, investors do have the option of investing in companies that support the industry rather than those producing the product directly. A few companies that fit this description include Scotts Miracle-Gro (NYSE: SMG) and GW Pharmaceuticals (NASDAQ:GWPH). Though it only makes up 10% of their revenue, Scotts Miracle-Gro acquired multiple hydroponics companies that serve the marijuana-growing industry. In addition, GW Pharmaceuticals' drugs Epidiolex and Sativex were produced using a formulated extract of the cannabis sativa plant. They sell it in 16 countries outside the United States to treat spasticity associated with multiple sclerosis.

## States where Marijuana is Legal

In the United States, the use of cannabis for medical purposes is legal in 30 states, plus the territories of Guam and Puerto Rico, and the District of Columbia, as of November 2017. These states include Alaska, Arizona, Arkansas, California, Colorado, Connecticut, Delaware, Florida, Hawaii, Illinois, Maine, Maryland, Massachusetts, Michigan, Minnesota, Missouri, Montana, Nevada, New

Hampshire, New Jersey, New Mexico, New York, North Dakota, Ohio, Oregon, Pennsylvania, Rhode Island, Utah, Vermont, and Washington.

Of those 30 states, 9 have legal recreational marijuana. These include Alaska, California, Colorado, Oregon, Massachusetts, Michigan, Nevada, Vermont and Washington.

Many more states are expecting to legalize in 2019, including New Jersey, Connecticut, Illinois, Minnesota, New Mexico, New York and Rhode Island.

# 2. Canada

The Canadian cannabis industry has continued to be a bright light for cannabis investors. Currently, Canada is the leading exporting hub for companies across the globe to obtain medical cannabis for use by patients in their respective countries. Canada currently exports medical cannabis to Australia, Brazil, Chile, Croatia, Germany, Jamaica, United States, New Zealand and more. The list is always growing.

## Full Legalization

After legalization of recreational marijuana in 2018, demand is so high right now, that supply in Canada is a real problem. With a completely legal market, licensed producers are reaping major profits. Canada sold C$43 million of legal pot in the first 2 weeks, with Ontario and Quebec accounting for half of the sales. A press release from Health Canada announced that the number of eligible enrollees in Canada's medical-weed program was growing by 10% a month!

As in previous years, Canadian stocks for the cannabis industry were super-hot in 2018. They reached a fever pitch by October 17th, the day in which Canada officially became the first G7 nation to legalize recreational marijuana with its new legislation. This first-world nation status adds greater credibility to the global marijuana marketplace.

In 2019, demand will continue to explode. Licensed producers have raised plenty of capital from investors who see the big picture. Companies like Canopy Growth (TSE:WEED) and Aphria Inc. (TSE: APH) have been aggressively expanding to increase production capacity. (seekingalpha.com)

**Licensed Producers**

Since legalization, there has been a shortage of cannabis, mostly because of the difficulty of becoming a licensed producer. Health Canada has approved not much more than 2 percent of applications thus far. Afterwards, in order to legally cultivate and sell cannabis in Canada, each company must be granted a license from Health Canada under the MMPR (Medical Purposes Regulations).

The LTB Licensed Producer Composite Index represents the most notable of these licensed producers, including: Aphria Inc. (OTCQB:APHQF), Aurora Cannabis (OTCQB:ACBFF), Canopy Growth (OTCPK:TWMJF), Emblem Corp. (OTCPK: EMMBF), Emerald Health (OTC:TBQBF), Mettrum Health (OTC:MQTRF), Organigram Holdings (OTCMKTS: OGRMF), PharmaCan Capital (OTC:PRMCF), Supreme Pharmaceuticals (OTCPK:SPRWF) and THC Biomed Int'l (OTCQB:THCBF).

## Buying Marijuana in Canada

Under the law, adults will be allowed to buy, use, possess and grow recreational marijuana. In Quebec and Alberta, the legal age is 18. For the remaining parts of the country, the age is 19. Furthermore, marijuana will not be sold in the same location as alcohol or tobacco.

"Consumers are expected to purchase the drug from retailers regulated by provinces and territories or from federally licensed producers when those options are not available." (CNN.com)

## Risks of Companies Investing in the U.S.

The Canadian Securities Administrators set out "specific disclosure expectations" for cannabis companies with investments in the U.S. The staff notice informed that these companies must tell investors about certain risks when they invest in the U.S., due to the prevalent laws against cannabis on the federal level. This includes the potential fallout if the legal landscape for cannabis changes. With this notice, operators of the Toronto Stock Exchange said it may also move to delist stocks of marijuana companies with operations in the United States. These "guidelines apply to all companies with U.S. marijuana-related activities, including direct and indirect involvement in growing and distribution, as well as those that provide goods and services to third parties involved in the U.S. industry." (cbc.ca/news)

Smartly, nearly all the Canadian companies listed in this book sell their marijuana products to countries all over the world (Germany, Mexico, South America, etc.)-- not just the U.S.

Back in 2017, major Canadian licensed producer, Aphria Inc. released a statement responding to both the CSA staff notice and the TSX guidance. "We believe the new CSA staff notice provides a very balanced framework for the Canadian capital markets," said CEO Vic Neufeld. "We welcome the additional guidance on specific and enhanced disclosure requirements for U.S. marijuana-related activities as they pertain to the medical marijuana industry in Canada." (fool.ca)

**Canada's Pricing and Tax**

One of the biggest concerns regarding Canada's marijuana legalization was pricing and taxation. After all, if legalized cannabis is too expensive, customers may turn to the black market. Quebec stores plan to have many strains available at around $7 or less in Canadian dollars (about $5.40 in US dollars) per gram to remain competitive with the black market.

Indeed, it has been competitive. Illegal drug dealers across the country have already responded by lowering their prices. Some in Montreal, for example, are offering two joints for the price of one.

A special marijuana excise tax, to be divvied up between the federal government and the provinces, will be included in the price; sales tax will be added at the cash register. These taxes are a lower rate than even alcohol in Canada. (nytimes.com)

# 3. Australia

In February of 2016, the Federal Government legalized the growing of cannabis for medicinal and scientific purposes at a federal level. Afterward, the use of medicinal cannabis was legalized by the Victorian government in April 2016, and in New South Wales in August 2016, the usage of medicinal cannabis became legal at the federal level on 1 November 2016, with implementation varying from state-to-state.

## Supply and Demand Issue

While not as far in the process as Canada, Australia is increasingly pro-medical marijuana. So much so, there is a big supply and demand problem. The government has indicated it's open to speeding things up, with Health Minister Greg Hunt recently announcing that authorities will allow more rapid importation of the commodity while a domestic supply is built. (theguardian.com)

## Canopy Growth to the Rescue

To counter delays for patients who have been prescribed medical cannabis, importers will now be allowed to buy from established suppliers overseas, then store it locally to be distributed via doctors. Mega Canadian weed producer, Canopy Growth Corporation (TSE: WEED) has this relationship with Australian company AusCann Group Holdings (ASX: AC8). According to AusCann Managing Director Elaine Darby, the agreement has cemented AusCann's leadership position in Australia's rapidly developing medicinal cannabis market. You can read more about Canopy Growth's rapid ascension and market dominance in the next chapter. (newcannabisventures.com)

## Proposal for Recreational Marijuana Legalization

For a brief moment in April 2018, marijuana users rallied around a proposal from the Greens party to legalize weed's use for recreational purposes in Australia.

But those hopes were shattered the next day, as Greg Hunt, the minister for health, said the government would oppose the plan. He believed Marijuana was a gateway to other drugs like methamphetamines.

"Our job is to protect the health of Australians. This action by the Greens risks the health of Australians." (nytimes.com)

## 4. Brazil

Recreational Cannabis in Brazil is still technically illegal, but possession and cultivation of personal amounts were decriminalized in 2006 and in 2017. Limited cannabis-based medicines are now permitted. In January, Brazil issued its first license for a cannabis-based medicine, allowing sales of an oral spray called Sativex by GW Pharmaceuticals.

### Legalization Coming Soon?

Brazil's Senate Social Affairs Committee approved a draft bill in November to legalize marijuana for medical use. This new bill would lift the penalties currently imposed for growing weed and would allow Brazilians to grow it for medicinal use, but only in amounts needed according to a medical prescription.

Senator Marta Suplicy believes the bill would make treatment more affordable for those enduring MS and epilepsy. Unfortunately, the bill faces political opposition. Other senate leaders are worried there won't be a sufficient method in tracking the amount of the drugs being produced.

The bill has many challenges before becoming law. Next, it will be under consideration by the full Senate and Brazil's Chamber of Deputies. On January 2019, president-elect Jair Bolsonaro is unfortunately expected to veto the bill.

## Bedrocan Brazil

Canopy Growth Corp., which owns Bedrocan, teamed up with Brazilian company Entourage Phytolab SA and founded a new subsidiary, Bedrocan Brazil. The latter imports products from Canopy Growth Corp. (TSE:WEED), while Entourage Phytolab SA will develop more medical cannabis products. (insiderfinancial.com)

When the market matures in South America, Bedrocan Brazil plans to produce and cultivate its own cannabis. But for now, it is importing from its Canadian parent company, Canopy Growth.

## HempMeds Brasil

Medical Marijuana Inc (OTCMKTS:MJNA) subsidiary HempMeds Brasil supported the launch of the Associação Nacional dos usuários de Canabidiol Patient Association in Brazil. This association is "committed to connecting people with cannabis-friendly physicians and continuing to update on the Brazilian medical community and its members on the therapeutic applications of cannabis." (mmjreporter.com)

# 5. Chile

In 2005, Chile formally decriminalized all cannabis use. Since 2014, Chile has allowed the cultivation of cannabis for medical purposes with the authorization of The Chilean Agriculture Service (SAG).

In 2016, a regulation bill was passed that now allows Chileans to grow small amounts of marijuana for medical, recreational or spiritual use. It was approved by the country's lower house of Congress.

## A Burgeoning Marijuana Industry

In an effort to bring more retailers, doctors and patients together with new technology, Grassroots SpA will become the exclusive distributor of technologies from Vancouver-based Global Cannabis Applications Corp.

Grassroots treats more than 3,000 patients across Chile. It will use GCAP's mobile applications, artificial intelligence and blockchain to better link doctors and patients.

"The cannabis market in Chile is where the Canadian market was five years ago: full of optimism and opportunity," said Alvaro Sequeida, president and chief executive at Grassroots. "We believe the Citizen Green Community platform, with its advanced technology, management dashboard and community-based approach, offers significant benefits to all involved in the Chilean medical cannabis market." (jurist.org)

**Fundación Daya**

AusCann (ASX: AC8), a licensed Australian producer entered into a joint-venture with Chilean group Fundación Daya-- the only group so far to have a medical cannabis production license in Chile. (seekingalpha.com)

**Chile's Neighbor Peru Also Legalizing**

In late 2017, lawmakers in Peru have voted overwhelmingly in favor of a bill to legalize medical marijuana, allowing cannabis oil to be locally produced, imported and sold. The medicinal use of cannabis is now legal in Peru, Colombia and Chile. In Uruguay, marijuana cultivation and use is permitted in all its forms.

# 6. Luxembourg

Sitting between France and Germany, Luxembourg is a small, liberal country of less than a million people. Despite its size and relative obscurity, this country made huge headlines this year within this space. It may in fact become only the third country—and the first in Europe-- to legalize recreational marijuana.

## Medicinal Weed Legalization

In June 2018, lawmakers in Luxembourg unanimously supported a bill to legalize medicinal marijuana. Passing on June 28, this law allows cannabis to be used by patients who suffer from a particular list of ailments, including muscle spasms, chronic pain, and nausea. The final version allows any doctor with relevant training to make prescriptions.

As with many countries on this list, the marijuana will be imported from Canada as oils and capsules, and only available from hospital pharmacies. (Luxembourg Times)

## The First EU Country to Legalize Recreational Marijuana?

According to the Consumer Choice Center (CCC), Luxembourg's three-party coalition government (Democrats, Socialists and the Greens) has announced it will legalize the recreational use of cannabis, as part of its manifesto for the next five years.

Bill Wirtz, a policy analyst at CCC, says "Early press statements by the coalition partners indicate that it would only be legal for residents. That would be the wrong way to go, since it is not only discriminatory but could also increase black market presence in the area.

"We feel that cannabis should be legal for purchase to all adults, regardless of nationality. Doing so could help create a new tourism industry in the country. At the end of the day, there is no reason to treat legal cannabis more strictly than legal alcohol. If foreigners, of age, can buy legal alcohol in the country, they should also be able to buy cannabis.

"The government should open a broad consultation process on the legalisation procedure. We want smart legalisation that benefits responsible consumers, helps ensure market-friendly regulations and will help protect the citizens of Luxembourg." (Luxembourg Times)

# 7. Czech Republic

Since 2010, possession of up to fifteen grams of cannabis for personal use or cultivation of up to five plants is a misdemeanor subject to minor fine. However, this is mostly not enforced. Medical use of cannabis on prescription has been legal and regulated since 2013. (wikipedia.org)

The Czech Republic has become a huge tourist attraction for marijuana enthusiasts, especially in Prague. As more and more countries begin to legalize recreational pot, they'll certainly do so as well to continue bringing in those tourists.

## MGC Pharmaceuticals

An Australian exchange listed cannabis company called MGC Pharmaceuticals is developing a library of medicinal cannabis research with the Royal Institute of Melbourne. They have a 5-year research partnership with Panax Pharma in the Czech Republic.

## Aurora Cannabis

Once again, a Canadian marijuana producer has been asked by a country to supply them with cannabis. This time, the lucky company is Aurora Cannabis Inc. (NYSE: ACB) (TSX: ACB) (Frankfurt: 21P; WKN: A1C4WM).

On November 27, 2018, Aurora announced that it had received an export request from the Czech Republic. Since then, Aurora has secured the required permits and has completed many shipments of medical cannabis to Czech Medical Herbs, a Czech pharmaceutical wholesaler.

"This supply arrangement demonstrates our ability to enter into new jurisdictions as the partner of choice in new markets with strong barriers to entry, and is testament to the strength and business execution of our European business development team," said Neil Belot, Chief Global Business Development Officer. "The Czech Republic represents the 21st country in which we operate, and exemplifies how we are rapidly expanding our global footprint in the medical cannabis space. We look forward to building a long-term relationship with our customer, CMH, and supplying patients in the Czech Republic with our high-quality cannabis products." (newswire.ca)

# 8. Ecuador

Production and distribution of cannabis in Ecuador is still prohibited. However, a movement is brewing as more and more public authorities are in favor of the non-criminalization of drug use in small doses. Ecuador is looking very closely to Uruguay, its neighboring country where it has regularized the marijuana market for years. It is not illegal to carry up to ten grams of cannabis in Ecuador. Despite the laws, police barely enforce them. (wikipedia.org)

Marijuana plants grow regularly in Ecuador due to its perfect climate for cultivation. The city of Cuenca in Ecuador is even known for their cannabis-infused chocolate, which give consumers a "mellow vibration." (Cuencahighlife.com)

**Ecuador Closer to Legalizing Marijuana**

Comprehensive health reform could potentially lead to cannabis finally being legalized. A legislative committee-- the National Assembly's standing commission on health-- approved the reform and it would lead to the production and manufacturing of medicinal marijuana throughout South America.

The cross-party committee of legislators calls the measure Libro II del Código de la Salud. It now moves to the full assembly.

Juan Pablo Bahamonde, director of UBG, an Ecuadoran company that specializes in health regulatory affairs, expects the bill to be law by mid-2019.

# 9. Germany

Germany is a cannabis-friendly country with a quarter of the population having consumed cannabis. That's almost 19 million people. Medical use became legal in 2017, along with a federal mandate for cheap access. German Health Minister, Hermann Gröhe, presented the legal draft on the legalization of medical cannabis to the cabinet, which took effect early in the year.

## For Ill Patients Only

The Cabinet of Germany approved the measure for legal medical cannabis for seriously ill patients who have consulted with a doctor and "have no therapeutic alternative". That means that public health insurance companies, which cover 90% of Germans, are on the front line of the cannabis efficacy issue. Consequently, Germany's medical market is potentially one of the most lucrative cannabis markets in the world, perhaps even rivaling California's recreational market. (CNN)

Recreational marijuana is still technically illegal in Germany, though laws are not enforced against people who are caught possessing less than 15 grams. Very similar to the United States, the law on marijuana consumption is decided in each of Germany's 16 federal states.

## Imported Marijuana

Germany is EU's most populous state with 82 million people. Yet at this time, it will rely entirely on imported marijuana for its patients. Canopy Growth Corporation (TSE:WEED) announced in November 2017 that it had entered into an agreement to acquire MedCann GmbH Pharma and Nutraceuticals (MedCann), a private pharmaceutical distributor in Germany. MedCann has already successfully placed Canopy Growth branded products in German pharmacies. Led by Dr. Pierre Debs, MedCann's team has established itself as a leading cannabis importer and distributor within Germany. (newcannabisventures.com)

Canadian LP, Aurora Cannabis Inc has become a top contender for cultivation in Germany, and has "quietly issued an ex-im license by both Canadian and German authorities. Publicly, this has been described as an effort to help stem the now chronic cannabis shortage facing patients who attempt to go through legitimate, prescribed channels. On the German side, intriguingly, this appears to be a provisional license." (cannabisindustryjournal.com)

## German Medical Cannabis Crops?

Germany's path to officially grow its own medical cannabis crops has not been a smooth one. In April 2017, the government released its bid at the ICBC conference, which held its first annual gathering in Berlin. The requirements of the bid was for a small amount of cannabis (2,000 kg), with "mandated experience producing high qualities of medical marijuana in a federally legitimate market. By definition that excluded all German hopefuls, and set up Canada and Holland as the only countries who could provide such experience, capital and backlog of crop as the growing gets started." (cannabisindustryjournal.com)

## 2018 Updates for the BfArM Cannabis Agency

On July 18th, the German Federal Institute for Drugs and Medical Devices (BfArM) set up a new one-step application process, in which applicants had until late October to participate in this new tender process.

One new requirement has been advantageous for many companies. In the first tender process, companies had to refer to exports in the production of medical marijuana. In the new tender process, it is now sufficient to just have experience in growing and processing medical marijuana.

In addition, the agency has further increased the quantity of weed that can be grown annually. Now, they have increased the amount for a period of four years to 2600 kilograms per year. (mjbizdaily.com)

# 10. Thailand

On December 25, 2018, another country surprisingly decided to join the green party. Thailand's interim parliament decided to amend the country's drug law to allow the licensed use of medicinal cannabis. However, recreational use of the drug will remain illegal.

Lawmaker Somchai Sawangkarn said the new amendment to the drug law "could be considered as a New Year gift to Thais."

"The amendment (on the Narcotics Bill) was passed the second and third readings today. And will become effective once it is published on the Royal Gazette."

The 166 members of the legislature voted in favor of the change unanimously, though 13 members abstained from voting. Once this new law takes effect, it will make Thailand the first country in Southeast Asia to legalize the use of medical marijuana. This is especially surprising considering Thailand is well known to be tough on drugs, including strict punishments for drug-related offenses. (cnn.com)

# 11. Israel

On March 5, 2017, Israel's Cabinet decriminalized the recreational use of marijuana, at its weekly meeting on Sunday in a move applauded by politicians from across the spectrum, left to right. The policy decriminalizes the illegal use of cannabis. However, growing and selling the plant would remain illegal. Not long after, 37 farmers received preliminary permits from the Health Ministry to construct facilities for the plant's cultivation. They will join an existing group of 8 medical-cannabis growers in the country.

Justice Minister Ayelet Shaked said in a statement, "Israel cannot shut its eyes to the changes being made across the world in respect to marijuana consumption and its effects." (CNN)

## Leading the Way in Research

Already a worldwide leader on marijuana-related research funded by the government, Israel's government has allowed medical marijuana as a tonic for intractable illnesses since 1992. Home to Raphael Mechoulam, the pioneer of marijuana research, Israel is where THC and the endocannabinoid system were first discovered. It has also become somewhat of a safe haven for American cannabis companies seeking to overcome federal roadblocks. In fact, one can argue that medical marijuana now being legal in 29 U.S. states and counting, is a direct result of Israeli research, which has in many way ways legitimized the study of cannabis.

## Lack of Supply

With pot legalization spreading like wildfire across globally, Israel believes marijuana can be a huge export for them. However, until Israel can ship medical marijuana to other countries within a few years, their biggest problem at the moment is a lack of supply. Consequently, Israel has lessened restrictions to allow more production facilities to grow and process weed.

The Israeli government has approved the export of medicinal marijuana products, enabling companies there to gain a sizable piece of the U.S. market. While importing cannabis into the United States is still federally illegal, companies can get around that ban by receiving drug approval from the FDA (Federal Drug Administration). According to the FDA, nothing is stopping them, as long as they meet the agency's strict requirements for approval.

"According to Saul Kaye, the founder of iCAN, an Israeli cannabis R&D firm, 2016 saw the investment of more than $250 million in Israeli cannabis companies and startups – half of that investment came from North America. Kaye predicts that investment will grow ten-fold over the next two years, reaching $1 billion. At least 50 American cannabis companies – and counting – have established R&D operations in Israel." (rollingstone.com)

Listed within the next chapter are 2 Israel-based publicly traded companies with plenty of potential. These companies are Teva Pharmaceuticals Industries (NYSE: TEVA) and One World Cannabis Ltd. (OTC: OWCP).

**New Bill Allowing Export Of Medical Marijuana**

On December 25, 2018, the Israeli Parliament (the "Knesset"), passed a new bill that will allow the export of medicinal cannabis to other countries.

This 16th amendment to Dangerous Drugs Ordinance concerns the regulations regarding the export of medical cannabis from Israel. Consequently, Israel is poised to become a global behemoth in the marijuana market, along with current leader Canada.

As we've seen with other countries, the measure was approved unanimously, followed by a positive vote by the Minister of Internal Security, Gilad Erdan, whose party is up for re-election.

The amendment also authorizes the Israeli Police to conduct supervision of cannabis farms, and grant approvals for the production and exporting of marijuana and marijuana-related products. Police involvement is essential for legality purposes. (cnn.com)

# 12. Jamaica

For many aficionados of the country, Red Stripe, Rum and Reggae are the main catalysts for taking a plane to Jamaica. However, for others who are more-in-the-know, a bigger attraction for tourists to the Caribbean island nation is to get your hands on what Jamaicans refer to as *Ganja*- aka marijuana.

## Early Stages

Jamaica is in the early stages of setting up a real medical cannabis industry. In early January, the Cannabis Licensing Authority granted conditional approval to three applicants for permits to cultivate and process marijuana. This comes almost a year after the passing of regulations to facilitate the cultivation of marijuana for medicinal, scientific, and therapeutic purposes.

On October 19, "Jamaica's Cannabis Licensing Authority has granted its first approvals for the nation's medical cannabis industry, as Everything Oily Labs Limited was issued a processing license and Epican was issued a license to cultivate," the Jamaica Gleaner reports.

Hyacinth Lightborne, chair of the CLA, indicated that 3 other applications were also approved, another 57 applicants are 'in the conditional approval stage,' and lastly, 209 other applications 'are currently being processed.' (ganjapreneur.com)

**Canopy Growth Corp Again**

Canopy Growth Corp. signed a deal to form a strategic partnership in Jamaica. The Canadian marijuana company says Jamaican company, Grow House JA Ltd. will now operate as Tweed Ltd JA. and serve the Jamaican medical cannabis market.

# 13. Mexico

On December 13, 2016, Mexico's senate voted to legalize medical marijuana, seeing potential for CBD. Earlier that year, patients in dire need were granted permits by the pressured Mexican Health Department to receive hemp-based CBD oil from overseas-- specifically a California-based company called HempMeds, a subsidiary of Medical Marijuana Inc (OTC: MJNA). This came after years of medical marijuana advocates pleaded on behalf of two Mexican families with children suffering from severe epilepsy.

"We, Mexicans know all too well the range and the defects of prohibitionist and punitive policies, and of the so-called war on drugs that has prevailed for 40 years," President Enrique Pena Nieto said. "Our country has suffered, as few have the ill effects of organized crime tied to drug trafficking. Fortunately, a new consensus is gradually emerging worldwide in favor of reforming drug policies. A growing number of countries are strenuously combating criminals, but instead of criminalizing consumers, they offer them alternatives and opportunities."

## Bill Finally Signed by Pena Nieto

In May 2017, the lower house of Mexico's Congress overwhelmingly passed the bill. Then on June 19, Mexican President Enrique Pena Nieto finally signed the bill into law.

The bill aims to classify the psychoactive component of cannabis tetrahydrocannabinol (THC) as a "therapeutic." Legalization of medical cannabis in Mexico would give pot-based businesses yet another avenue to legally sell their product beyond Canada and the United States. HempMeds continues its partnership with the Mexican Health Department. For most of 2017, it sold the only legal cannabis-based products allowed into Mexico.

According to Stuart Titus, the CEO of Medical Marijuana, Inc., legalizing medical marijuana in Mexico represents a "$1 billion to $2 billion opportunity" in cumulative revenue over the next decade, according to an interview with Fortune.

## 2018 Supreme Court Decision

On October 31, 2018, Mexico's Supreme Court ruled individuals can use cannabis under their right to decide their own recreational activities. In other words, the court deemed the country's current prohibition law is unconstitutional. The decision places the country a whole lot closer to full legalization.

It was not the first time the court made such a decision. However, under the country's laws, once the Supreme Court reaches a similar decision in five separate cases, the rulings apply to the country's entire court system.

The ruling, while not fully legalizing marijuana, does allow individuals to press his or her case in the judicial system. In essence, the ruling deems that total marijuana prohibition is unconstitutional.

# 14. New Zealand

After alcohol and tobacco, marijuana is already the third most widely used recreational drug in New Zealand, and the most widely used illegal drug. According to the World Drug Report, this ranks as the ninth highest cannabis consumption level in the world. The use of marijuana in New Zealand is governed by the Misuse of Drugs Act 1975, which makes unauthorized possession of any amount of cannabis illegal.

In March 2016, New Zealand's Associate Health Minister Peter Dunne stated he would back policy changes regarding medical marijuana if it is proven to be effective in treating illnesses.

## Marijuana Referendum

After nine years of conservative rule, liberal Jacinda Ardern was confirmed as the nation's next prime minister on October 19, 2017. Ardern promptly announced she would hold a referendum on whether to legalize recreational marijuana at some point over the next 3 years. She did not mention if she personally favored legalization.

"I've always been very open about the fact that I do not believe that people should be imprisoned for personal use of cannabis," Ardern said. "On the flip side, I also have concerns around young people accessing a product which

can clearly do harm and damage to them."
(washingtonpost.com)


## 2018 Law Making Weed Widely Available

A nationwide referendum on recreational pot is planned within two years.

After years of campaigning by chronically sick New Zealanders, the government has issued a law that will make cannabis available for thousands of patients without the possibility of penalty. This includes allowing terminally ill patients to use marijuana immediately, since for them, it may be the only thing that eases their pain.

The law would also enable New Zealand companies to manufacture medicinal marijuana products for both the local and international market, an industry which is clearly booming. As in the U.S. and Canada, New Zealand hopes to turn the thriving black market into a booming legal market.

The health minister, David Clarke says, "People nearing the end of their lives should not have to worry about being arrested or imprisoned for trying to manage their pain. This is compassionate and caring legislation that will make a real difference to people … They can use illicit cannabis without fear of prosecution."

There is also a referendum on recreational marijuana use. The government has pledged to hold the referendum within two years. The opposition National party slammed the move as "lazy and dangerous".

"We support medicinal cannabis but strongly oppose the smoking of loose leaf cannabis in public. Smoked loose leaf is not a medicine," said the Nationals' spokesperson on health, Shane Reti.

Chronically ill patients will still have to wait a year before using marijuana-- when a fresh set of legislation will be put into place. (washingtonpost.com)

# 15. Portugal

In 2001, Portugal became the first country ever to decriminalize the use of all drugs– making possession of personal quantities of all drugs, including cannabis, a non-criminal offence. Since then, Portugal has experienced major benefits, including a decrease in "hard" drug use and drug related crimes. (forbes.com)

However, in 2003, an amendment was made that criminalized the sale and possession of any cannabis seed not certified as of a European hemp variety. This mostly means Portugal is largely opposed to cultivation, even banning the sale of equipment intended for cultivation. Furthermore, Portugal's neighboring country of Spain has such a well-developed cannabis market that many users in Portugal rely on cannabis grown in Spain or imported from Morocco. This is especially true in the case of hashish.

In 2017, Portugal continually decriminalized possession of marijuana by softening up its laws. So much so, that in September, Canadian marijuana producers finally acquired a license from the Portuguese government to import cannabis seeds and clones. This is a major win for Canadian investors, as it will open up a whole new market in Europe.

**New 2018 Cannabis Law Opens Domestic Market**

In June, lawmakers approved changes to the current laws that regulate the use of marijuana. This includes regulations for cultivation, manufacturing and distribution.

This will open up new markets for international companies, specifically Tilray (NASDAQ: TLRY). Last year, the Canada-based Tilray set up a $22 million medical marijuana production facility in Portugal to serve the European Union. Tilray CEO Brendan Kennedy said that given its warm weather, "Portugal seemed like the ideal location to grow plants." (greencamp.com)

The National Authority of Medicines and Health Products will be in charge of most of these new regulations, with all products now requiring a license from the government agency and only being available through pharmacies and prescriptions.

The law went into effect July 1, but the market is just now being open for business—the beginning of 2019. (nytimes.com)

# 16. Puerto Rico

In 2015 the Governor of Puerto Rico signed an executive order to legalize cannabis for medicinal use only.

Governor Garcia-Padilla said in a statement to the press: "We're taking a significant step in the area of health that is crucial to our development and high expectations for their quality of life. I am sure that many patients will receive appropriate treatment that will offer them new hope." (fortaleza.pr.gov)

## Government Learning Curve Issues

In 2017, medical marijuana dispensaries in Puerto Rico began operating for the first time in the U.S. territory. However, the Puerto Rican government has not made the process easy for everyone. Patients, tourists, and business owners are all having trouble operating within the current system. There are over 11,000 patients in Puerto Rico awaiting their patient ID cards. There just isn't enough employees processing applications and not enough places for patients to submit and receive their paperwork. (hightimes.com)

## Market Growing Exponentially in 2018

A year after two hurricanes devastated the beautiful island of Puerto Rico and killed 3,000 people, medical marijuana businesses are reporting an amazing turnaround.

Mostly due to the horrifying strength of Hurricane Maria, cannabis cultivation, manufacturing and retail facilities were completely destroyed with companies racking up millions of dollars in damages in leveled greenhouses and rebuilding costs. Many businesses had to start completely from scratch.

The good news is that Puerto Rico marijuana growers seem to have caught up with the demand. A growing list of patients—about 50,000-- are in need of the medicinal crop. That's up from 12,000 last year. (losangelestimes.com)

# 17. South Africa

Early in 2017, medical marijuana, known as dagga to South Africans, was approved by the country's government. Dr. Mario Oriani-Ambrosini created the Medical Innovation Bill in 2014, which proposed the complete legalization of medical and recreational cannabis. After being diagnosed with stage IV lung cancer, Dr. Oriani-Ambrosini became a major advocate for the legalization of cannabis before his death in August 2014. (merryjane.com)

## Regulation on the Way

The Medical Control Council, South Africa's medical regulatory agency that uses a variety of experts to evaluate the distribution and marketing of medicine, is in the process of forming new guidelines for the production of cannabis oil and other cannabis products.

Recently, the ban on using cannabis recreationally is being challenged in the High Court, which raised the possibility that it would be effectively decriminalized some time in 2019. (mg.co.za)

## Supreme Court Legalizes the Private Use of Marijuana

South Africa's top court unanimously legalized the private use of cannabis in September 2018. The decision was made to uphold a lower court's decision, in which criminalizing marijuana was deemed to be invalid and unconstitutional. Specifically, the ruling allows adults to grow and consume marijuana for private consumption.

"It will not be a criminal offense for an adult person to use or be in possession of cannabis in private for his or her personal consumption," Deputy Chief Justice Raymond Zondo wrote in his judgment.

The Supreme Court has given parliament about 2 years to adopt the ruling, which is already binding. It should be noted however, that using, selling and supplying cannabis in public is still illegal. (BBC)

## 18. Poland

On July 24, 2017, Poland's Lower House of Parliament overwhelmingly voted to legalize medical marijuana. A recommendation from the nation's Health Care Committee helped enormously. The bill was authored by MP Piotr Liroy-Marzec, who has long been an advocate for the legalization of medical cannabis. Liroy-Marzec's original proposal would have allowed Polish citizens to cultivate their own medical cannabis. However, Polish legislators dropped that provision, instead opting in favor of a regulatory system. Therefore, Polish patients will rely on a limited number of medical cannabis exporters, most likely from licensed producers in Canada. (newcannabisventures.com)

In November 2017, it became official that imported plants can now be used to make prescription drugs in Polish pharmacies. The bill took effect that October. It allowed medical marijuana to be prescribed in many forms, including tinctures and resin.

The Polish Pharmaceutical Chamber estimates that "up to 300,000 patients" could qualify for medical marijuana. "The law is unrestrictive, giving doctors leeway to prescribe marijuana to any medical condition if its usefulness is supported by research." (konbini.com)

### Aurora Cannabis as Medical Marijuana Supplier

Canadian producer, Aurora Cannabis (NYSE:ACB) announced in a news release that it had received an "Ok" to ship medical marijuana to Poland. Poland's market has suffered from a lack of supply, due to it being illegal to cultivate the crop domestically.

This will make the Alberta company the first non-government-run business to import marijuana products to the eastern European country. (mjbizdaily.com)

## 19. Italy

Marijuana for medical or religious purposes is legal here, but still illegal if used for recreational purposes. The country first legalized medical marijuana in 2007.

Getting caught with even small amounts of marijuana for personal use can still land you a misdemeanor. However, Liberties.eu reports that it's more likely you will just pay a fine, especially if you are a first time offender.

Cannabis businesses have been so successful that growers have actually complained about not being able to keep up with demand. Earlier this year, several political groups began a movement to legalize recreational marijuana. They've collected over 68,000 signatures, but the national government has not yet discussed a proposal. (forbes.com)

# 20. Greece

In July 2017, Greece announced a new law permitting the use of medical marijuana. Prime Minister Alexis Tsipras stated that medical professionals in Greece will soon be able to prescribe cannabis for various medical conditions.

Health Minister Andreas Xanthos announced in May that medical cannabis preparations could be manufactured and packaged soon, although the exact guidelines for this process are still to be determined. If deemed necessary, production, packaging, and marketing for Greece will be developed by the state, Xanthos emphasized. (marijuana.com)

## Greece Approves Core Legislature for Medical Cannabis

In March 2018, the Greek Legislature approved legislation for medicinal marijuana. "A joint ministerial decision later defined the application process and facility requirements, while the Ministry of Health outlined the market authorization process." (mjbizdaily.com)

More recently, in November, Greece issued its first licenses to grow medicinal marijuana to two privately owned companies. This will in turn open cultivation and manufacturing opportunities for international and domestic medical cannabis companies.

Bioprocann S.A is one of the companies that was awarded the license. It intends to cultivate in a 21,500-square-foot indoor area and 64,500 square feet of greenhouse space.

"Exporting is definitely part of our current vision and our strategic approach," Nikolas Onoufriadis, a principal at Bioprocann.

Currently, Greece's laws regarding marijuana products allows for exports as long as the receiving country holds the required import license.

# The 18 Best Globally Traded Marijuana Companies

## Overview

For reasons this book illustrated earlier, most of the best publicly traded pot companies do not reside in the United States where much uncertainty still prevails. You will find the bulk of the fastest growing marijuana companies are listed in the exchanges of foreign countries, like Canada.

Since Canada has made recreational marijuana legal in 2018, a number of new Canadian companies have risen to meet the challenge of satisfying an exponentially growing demand in 2019— Not just in Canada, but the many other countries listed above who desperately need their exported products. This has made Canada the leading export of marijuana-related products. Consequently, not only does this year's edition of our ebook list more Canadian companies than ever, these companies are also powerhouses that are already starting to be listed on top US exchanges like Nasdaq and the NYE.

With the help of the brokers listed previously in this book, investors will find that it's just as easy to get a piece of the pot action in Canada and in any other foreign country as it is in their own country. As a reminder, with top brokerages like Interactive Brokers, shares in these companies can be bought in the American over-the-counter (OTC) markets or directly from its original exchange. This is why each listed stock below will have ticker symbols listed for 2 markets-- its native exchange and its version on the OTC market. For instance, Canopy Growth Corporation has the ticker WEED on the TSE exchange. However, on the OTC market, its ticker is TWMJF. With either one, you are at the mercy of the prevailing currency rate, so do your due diligence before trading.

The companies on the next page were listed based on technical and fundamental analysis, market share, partnerships and strong leadership that have led to dozens of triple-digit profits over the past few years.

In addition, make no mistake, there will be plenty more publicly-traded companies coming in 2019. The last section of this chapter includes a small list of the marijuana-related companies that will likely IPO in 2019. More often than not, the prices of a stock on its Initial Public Offering are the best prices you will ever see.

Lastly, remember that past performance is no guarantee of success. Without further delay, here's the definitive list of the best, safest, fastest growing companies in the pot biz.

# The Stocks

## 1. Canopy Growth Corporation (TSE:WEED) (CGC:NYSE)

Founded by Bruce Linton on August 5, 2009 and headquartered in Smith Falls, Canada. Canopy Growth Corporation supplies an unmatched selection of premium medical marijuana, with exposure to ever-growing markets in Canada, U.S., Germany, Denmark, Australia, Jamaica, South America and much more.

### Incredible Growth

The company has recorded strong growth on pretty much all metrics and at the end of 2018, Canopy Growth reported to have around 100,000 registered patients which is more than double over the previous year. After Canada officially legalized the recreational market in Canada in 2018, Canopy Growth's stock price hit amazing highs of $50 U.S. dollars!

Last year, Canopy Growth emerged as the most dominant medical marijuana supplier in the world. It also ingeniously changed its TSX ticker to WEED, made profound partnerships with recognizable brands and announced its acquisition of Mettrum Health Corp. which gives it plenty of leverage to capitalize on recreational use in Canada and eventually the United States. (nasdaq.com)

## Revenue

Canopy's last 2018 quarter earnings report featured numerous highlights. Most recently, revenue was $60.7 million, over a 300% increase over last year.

Some revenue was understandably lost as Canopy subsidiaries Mettrum, Tweed and Bedrocan were mostly made inactive through 2018. This was because they were integrated with new standard quality control procedures, as well as being launched into the Tweed Main Street online store.

CEO Bruce Linton, "Recording sales of $1M in a single day earlier this year revealed many points in our sales, fulfillment and shipping infrastructure that needed strengthening. With many customers asking to be able to access all products under the canopy, it made perfect sense for us to transition, in April, from multiple, single brand sites to the Tweed Main Street marketplace. Bringing all products of our many leading brands together under one roof, to provide a shopping experience similar to what customers expect in many other markets, has strengthened our leadership position."

Since 2014, the revenue has grown about 5000% making it the fastest growing LP in Canada. The revenue for Canopy is expected to increase at a rate of about 200% annually and the earnings at a rate of 142% quarterly. No wonder it was the first billion dollar Marijuana stock.

**2019 Earnings**

Canopy Growth Corporation is estimated to report next earnings on 02/13/2019. In that report, Wall Street analysts expect CGC to have year-over-year growth of 18.18%. Meanwhile, the latest consensus estimate is calling for revenue of $73.90 million, up 332.42% from the prior-year quarter. (Nasdaq.com)

Extrapolation of these figures produces $25 billion revenue potential and $7.5 billion operating profit potential within a decade. It's not hard to imagine Canopy Growth Corporation eventually being worth around $100 billion in a decade.

**Expansion**

With its aggressive expansion, Canopy has been developing up to three million square feet of greenhouse growing capacity in British Columbia. This facility will help Canopy significantly scale up the production footprint. (smallcappower.com)

Canopy Growth also acquired German marijuana distributor MedCann, giving it a major distribution network in Europe. This will ultimately put Canopy Growth (Tweed-branded) cannabis strains into pharmacies in Germany, where medical marijuana has been legal since 2005. With a highly experienced leadership team, led by Dr. Pierre Debs, MedCann has established itself as a leading marijuana importer and distributor within Germany where the cannabis industry still relies solely on imports.

In addition, Canopy Growth announced an export deal with Brazil. Their wholly owned subsidiary, Bedrocan Canada Inc., completed their first ever export of dried cannabis from Canada to Brazil. Canopy hopes to work towards building a solidified medicinal cannabis platform in Brazil. (seekingalpha.com)

As mentioned in the last section, Canopy Growth Corp. also signed a deal to form a strategic partnership in Jamaica. The Canadian marijuana company says Jamaican company, Grow House JA Ltd. (in which Canopy has a 49% stake) will now operate as Tweed Ltd JA. and serve the Jamaican medical cannabis market. Tweed JA has conditional license approvals and has begun construction of its facility. (bnn.ca)

Canopy Growth also expanded its production capacity in Canada by around 1.1 million square feet. Canopy Growth's expansion means the company has now established a 5.6 million square feet for production.

Its marketing efforts include a partnership with famously pro-pot supporter and musician Snoop Dog.

**Fortune 500 Company Stake**

In 2018, Constellation Brands, Inc., a Fortune 500 company that owns brands such as Corona beer, Black Velvet Whisky and Casa Noble tequila agreed to take a 9.9% stake in Canopy Growth Corporation. The two companies are working together to develop and market beverages that will be infused with Cannabis. (wsj.com)

## Conclusion

In order to justify Canopy Growth Corporation's amazing ascent and acquire new investors, management will need to boost sales enough to offset its costly expansion projects. However, keep in mind, a company at its stage of development should be spending on future growth anyway. Not giving back to shareholders. Nevertheless, Canopy Growth is establishing a worldwide presence amid a shift toward greater acceptance of marijuana use.

Visit canopygrowth.com for more current information.

## Company Highlights (as of December 30, 2018)

Market Capitalization: $9.4 B

Shares Outstanding: 342.7 M

Revenue: $60.7 M

Industry: Agricultural Commodities/ Milling

Share Price 52 Week Range: $16.74 - 59.25

# Company Profile

Address: 1 Hershey Drive, Smith Falls, Ontario K7A 0A8

Phone: +1.855.558.9333

Number of Employees: 1033

Chairman: Bruce Linton

Chief Operating Officer & Director: Cole Cacciavillani

Chief Financial Officer & Senior Vice President: Timothy R. Saunders

Managing Director: Mark Zekulin

# 2. Aurora Cannabis Inc. (TSE: ACB) (NYE: ACB)

Another licensed producer with a market cap in excess of $5 billion, Aurora Cannabis Inc. is headquartered in Vancouver, Canada. Its medical cannabis products include Borealis Blend, Odin, Odin 3, Peechee, Sentinel, Stokes, and Warwick 2. Aurora's product types include Tetrahydrocannabinol (THC), Cannabidiole (CBD), Indica, Sativa and hybrid.

Aurora operates in 22 countries and holds partnership agreements with several drug retail chains for the distribution, sale, and marketing of medicinal marijuana products. Aurora also operates a network of counseling centers called CanvasRX. CanvasRX offers marijuana medical treatment for its patients.

Canopy Growth Corp. remains ahead of Aurora on our list because it has the advantage of its branding, many export deals and a first-mover position in the market. However, with its strong fundamentals, partnerships and expansion deals, Aurora may overtake Canopy by the end of 2019.

## Revenue

Recently, the Canada-based Marijuana company reported fiscal quarter net earnings that rose to C$105.5 million from C$3.6 million a year ago, and from C$79.9 million in the previous quarter. Total revenue rose 260% from a year ago and 55% from the previous quarter to C$29.7 million, while cannabis revenue jumped 236% from last year and 65% from last quarter to C$24.6 million.

The average selling price per gram of dried cannabis grew 15% from a year ago to C$8.39, while the cash cost per gram fell 12% to C$1.90. For cannabis extracts, the net selling price per gram fell 26% to C$12.12, while costs declined 22% to C$1.45. Active registered patients rose 250% to 67,484. The jump in net earnings was primarily attributable to unrealized non-cash gains on derivatives and marketable securities. (Nasdaq.com)

## Expansion

As has been mentioned many times in this book, the Canadian legalization of marijuana this past year for recreational use has further drove up demand. With its low-cost production, Aurora is so far meeting the demands of both the medical and anticipated recreational opportunities. Meeting customer demand has been an issue that many companies in the industry have faced. However, Aurora has been building their inventory since 2016 in an effort to gain market share from competitors like the Canopy and Aphria.

Aurora Cannabis secured a nearly 20% stake in Cann Group, a publicly traded Australian company. Cann Group is the first company in Australia to be licensed for the cultivation and research of medicinal cannabis. With this smart investment, Aurora found its way into more markets, especially the rapidly developing Australian market. (streetregister.com)

Aurora Cannabis also raised an additional $60 million through equity bought deal financings to further its aggressive expansion, as well as to fund its international growth program. Given the significant demand for this bought deal financing, Aurora agreed to raise another $6 million. After this development, Aurora Cannabis acquired about $200 million in cash to help with its expansion goals. (smallcappower.com)

Aurora announced it had received all the required permits to ship dried cannabis flower from Canada to Germany. This enabled the company to begin supplying the German medical marijuana market through its wholly-owned subsidiary Pedanios GmbH ("Pedanios"), Germany's top medical cannabis distributor. (newswire.ca)

What makes Aurora's recent earnings even more special is that the last quarter did not include revenue from its CanniMed acquisition (completed in May 2018), and none of its MedReleaf transaction (completed in July 2018). Lastly, rumors are brewing regarding a possible partnership with the Coca-Cola Company to develop cannabis-infused beverages.


## Mexican Importer

Aurora recently bought out Farmacias Magistrales. Farmacias made news in 2018 when it became the first and sole Mexican importer of raw marijuana products that contain THC.

This buyout allows Aurora Cannabis a profitable channel to Latin America's medical-marijuana market. Besides Farmacias, Aurora also has operations in Colombia and Uruguay. (seekingalpha.com)

## Conclusion

Over the past two years, Aurora Cannabis has gained 196.5% compared to a gain of 11.1% for the S&P 500. 2018 was a great year for Aurora, as it transformed itself into a fully integrated company, giving them control over the entire process – from production to sales, as well as diversifying their operations.

Investors are excitedly investing in this marijuana producer, with the potential to provide enormous returns now that recreational legalization is a reality. With so much cash on the books, aggressive expansion and an ever increasing revenue, Aurora Cannabis Inc. is looking to be Canada's top licensed pot producer.

Visit auroramj.com for more current information.

# Company Highlights (as of December 30, 2018)

Market Capitalization: $5.2 B

Shares Outstanding: 997.9 M

Revenue: $43.5 M

Industry: Agriculture/ Milling

Share Price 52 Week Range: $4.05 - 12.53


# Company Profile

Address: 10355 Jasper Avenue, Edmonton, Alberta T5J 1Y6

Phone: +1.855.279.4652

Number of Employees: 967

Chief Executive Officer & Non-Independent Director: Terry Booth

President & Director: Steve Dobler

Chief Financial Officer: Glen W. Ibbott

Executive Vice President: Cam Battley

# 3. Tilray Inc. (NASDAQ:TLRY)

Tilray, Inc. engages in the research, cultivation, production, and distribution of medical cannabis and cannabinoids. Its products include dried cannabis and cannabis extracts. The company was founded on January 24, 2018 and is headquartered in Nanaimo, Canada.

Tilray is the most interesting company on this list. It is first marijuana producing company to IPO on a major American stock exchange. Within just a few months after its IPO, TLRY stock momentarily went up a whopping 1000%! Since then, shares stabilized near the $70 level.

## Revenue

Tilray reported net losses of $18.7 million for the third quarter of 2018, which amounts to 20 cents a share, widening from $1.8 million, or 2 cents a share, in the year-earlier period. Tilray's sales and marketing expenses more than doubled compared to a year ago. General and administrative expenses also went up substantially as Tilray got ready for Canadian's full legalization of recreational marijuana. (Nasdaq.com)

## Expansion

In 2018, Tilray made many investments and acquisitions. the company invested C$7.5M In December, Tilary announced an investment in Québec-based cannabis producer, ROSE LifeScience Inc. ("ROSE") and an exclusive sale, supply, distribution and marketing agreement between High Park Farms Ltd. ("High Park"), a wholly-owned subsidiary of Tilray, and ROSE.

Also recently, Tilray Canada Ltd., a subsidiary of Tilray Inc signed a global collaboration agreement with Sandoz AG, a leading pharmaceutical company to increase availability of high quality medical marijuana-related products globally.

AB InBev, the global leader in brewing, also decided to partner with Tilray to research non-alcohol beverages containing THC and CBD. This research partnership combines AB InBev's profound experience with the beverage industry with Tilray's growing expertise in marijuana products.

## Conclusion

The significance of Tilray becoming the first marijuana company on a major US exchange is not lost on most investors. The IPO process in the United States is universally considered to be very rigorous. Many disclosures and external auditing are required. An United States IPO has given Tilray more credibility from international investors than most of the companies listed in this chapter.

Visit www.tilray.com/ for more current information.

## Company Highlights (as of December 30, 2018)

Market Capitalization: $5.7 B

Shares Outstanding: 76.5 M

Revenue: $20.5 M

Industry: Biotechnology

Share Price 52 Week Range: $20.10 - 300.00

## Company Profile

Address: 1100 Maughan Road, Nanaimo, British Columbia V9X IJ2

Phone: +1.844.845.7291

Number of Employees: 245

President, Chief Executive Officer & Director: Brendan Kennedy

Chief Financial Officer, Secretary & Treasurer: Mark Castaneda

Chief Science Officer & Vice President: Joshua Eades

# 4. Cronos Group, Inc. (TSE: CRON) (NASDAQ: CRON)

Formerly known as PharmaCan Capital Corp, Cronos Group Inc. invests in firms which are licensed to produce and sell medical marijuana. Its portfolio includes In The Zone, Peace Naturals, Whistler Medical Marijuana Co., ABcann, Hydropothecary, Vert Medical, and Evergreen Medicinal Supply. Its Peace Naturals subsidiary is already exporting to Germany.

The company was founded by Lorne Michael Gertner and Paul Rosen on August 21, 2012 and is headquartered in Toronto, Canada.

## Earnings

The major cannabis producer enjoyed a strong second quarter in 2018. Revenue and earnings surged. However, the recent third-quarter had mixed results. While the company continued to report solid sales, with revenue soaring to 186% over last year and almost 11% higher than the second quarter, Cronos also reported a net loss of about $5.5 million.

The loss is mostly due to operating expenses, as they increased about 242% year over year. These expenses were expected since Cronos had to ramp up production for the beginning of the recreational marijuana market in Canada.

These expenses—as like any investment—should yield a profitable return in the long term.

## Expansion

In 2018, Cronos completed Building 4 at its Peace Naturals facility in Stayner, Ontario. This building adds another 286,000 square feet to its production facilities. Once operating at its peak, Cronos Group should be able to produce around 40,000 kg of cannabis per year. In total, Cronos is projected to boost annual production capacity to over 117,000 kilograms within the next few years. (fool.com)

Most of the recent investor optimism for Cronos came after the announced partnership with tobacco company, Altria Group (NYSE: MO). The deal provides Cronos with a nice stash of cash to further develop its CBD products. For Altria, the company gets to innovate its own products within this new growing market. For instance, Altria has attempted to break into the vaporizer market with its own heat-not-burn tobacco products. With Cronos' expertise in CBD, Altria may succeed.

Cronos also formed a partnership with Pedanios to export cannabis to Germany. In an interview on Bezinga.com, CEO Michael Gorenstein stated, "We see Germany and other places in Europe as extremely attractive [markets] because cannabis is treated as a medicine. Like any other medicine, you receive a prescription for it from your doctor, and insurance is mandated to cover it," Gorenstein added. "That, I believe, is what separates it from other places where everyone is wondering when will recreational legalization come. I believe an insurance-covered medical market is at least as good, if not superior, to a recreational market."

Lastly, Cronos also recently announced partnerships with Ginkgo Bioworks to assist with cultivation and Colombian agricultural company Agroidea SAS in a deal that'll open doors to the growing South American market. (thecronosgroup.com)

## Conclusion

Investors are paying lots of attention to Cronos and how it grows over the long term. With competition as stiff as it can be, its success increasingly hinges on its production capacity, its distribution channels (both in Canada and in international markets), and its innovation. Cronos is meeting those goals nicely and will likely continue to in 2019. (newswire.ca/)

Visit thecronosgroup.com for more current information.

# Company Highlights (as of December 30, 2018)

Market Capitalization: $1.9 B

Shares Outstanding: 178.7 M

Revenue: $3.1 M

Industry: Agriculture

Share Price 52 Week Range: $4.75 - 15.30


# Company Profile

Address: 720 King Street West, Toronto, Ontario M5V 2T3

Phone: 416-504-0004

Number of Employees: 107

Chairman, Chief Executive Officer, President: Michael Gorenstein J.D.

Chief Financial Officer: William Hilson CPA

Chief Operating Officer: David Hsu

# 5. Aphria Inc. (NYE: APHA) (TSE:APH)

Aphria, Inc. is a top Canadian licensed producer engaging in the production and supply of medical marijuana. At the time of this writing, its share price over the last 12 months had soared upwards of 500% to a market cap in excess of $1 billion. Along with other top licensed producers in Canada, Aphria outperformed 94% of TSE-listed stocks in the same period. The company was founded by Cole Cacciavillani and John Cervini on June 22, 2011 and is headquartered in Leamington, Canada.

Aphria was #1 on our list in last year's edition of this ebook. However, the competition—including Aurora, Canopy Growth and Tilray—expanded quicker, had larger increases in share price and reported more exponential revenue. However, as the saying goes, slow and steady often wins the race.

## Revenue

Aphria reported solid revenue growth in first quarter of 2019. The company announced an increase in the amount of grams sold, higher gross profit and lower product costs. Canadian-based production capacity on schedule to reach 255,000kg per year. Aphria also signed supply agreements with every province in Canada and the Yukon Territory. This means 99% of Canada's population has access to Aphria's products.

In the final full quarter, Aphria also announced an agreement to be the exclusive sales representative for We Grow BC Ltd. The companies included in their portfolio include Solei Sungrown Cannabis, RIFF, Good Supply, and Goodfields.

"Aphria started fiscal 2019 by taking significant steps to solidify our position as a premier global cannabis company," said Vic Neufeld, Chief Executive Officer, Aphria. "We advanced the build out of our expansion in Leamington, signed coast-to-coast supply agreements, launched our strong portfolio of adult-use brands, and created strategic collborations with leading companies like Perennial that will ensure Aphria continues to lead the consumer experience as the cannabis industry evolves."

"Going forward, we are well positioned not only for the recreational market in Canada, but also the continued growth and leadership of the medical cannabis market globally. With committed supply agreements, a substantial and growing production footprint, a diversified brand portfolio, proven product development and innovation capabilities, and strong international alliances, Aphria is focused on driving sustainable long-term profitable growth and capitalizing on the most accretive cannabis opportunities around the world." (aphria.com)

No other Canadian producer is lowering costs like Aphria. The cost of producing a gram of dried cannabis decreased 14.4% from the 4th quarter to $0.95 per gram. The excellent ratio between revenue growth and production costs allowed Aphria to drive gross profits before fair value adjustments up 43.7% to $4.77 million. If they continue to head in that direction, they may pull away from the competition.

## Expansion

Aphria's decreasing production costs are mostly due to its expansion efforts. In 2018, Aphria completed a 1,000,000-square-foot cannabis cultivation facility that increased output to 70,000 kg of dried cannabis anually. The facility includes more greenhouse space and warehouse areas. With this increased capacity, production costs should continue to go down as their supply increases to meet the high demand. Aphria's total annual cannabis output should increase to 255,000 kg by May 2019.

## Investments

Aphria has a large portion of its investments in the North American cannabis industry mostly through its stake in Liberty Health Services. Aphria's investments include companies Canabo Medical, CannaRoyalty, Copperstate Farms, Green Acre Capital, Kalytera Therapeutics, MassRoots, Resolve Digital Health and Scythian BioSciences.

Aphria also provides consultative services to Nuuvera in return for a piece of the company's sales. Their deal is estimated to be at least $10 million a year once production is achieved; which should drive Aphria's net profits even higher. (aphria.com)

**Green Growth's Offer**

Most recently, retail company Green Growth Brands (OTCQB: GGBXF) offered to swap GGBXF shares for all outstanding shares of Aphria-- at $8 per share of Aphria stock, which actually represents an almost 50% increase over Aphria's 2018 closing price. The deal would value Aphria at $2.1 billion U.S. dollars.

Green Growth's offer is based on combining the Schottenstein family's long experience in the retail business with Aphria's ability to grow lots of pot.

**Conclusion**

Aphria's management has smartly scaled the company with the growth of the industry, as opposed to building too fast. With recreational cannabis now fully legalized in Canada, Aphria has put itself in an advantageous position, ensuring it will be a market leader in the Canadian cannabis market for years to come.

Visit www.aphria.com/ for more current information.

# Company Highlights (as of December 30, 2018)

Market Capitalization: $1.6 B

Shares Outstanding: 249.8 M

Revenue: $29.0 M

Net Profit Margin: 80.93%

Industry: Pharmaceuticals

Share Price 52 Week Range: $3.75 - 19.87


# Company Profile

Address: 245 Talbot Street West, Leamington, Ontario N8H 1N8

Phone: +1.844.427.4742

Number of Employees: 300

Chairman, President & Chief Executive Officer: Victor Neufeld

Chief Operating Officer & Director: Cole Cacciavillani

Chief Financial Officer: Carl A. Merton

President: Jakob Ripshtein

# 6. GW Pharmaceuticals (NASDAQ:GWPH)

Based in the U.K., there's a very good chance that GW Pharmaceuticals could be consistently profitable by 2020 with its endeavors in cannabis-related medicinal products. With a market cap of $2.4 billion, GW Pharmaceuticals is a drug development company that focuses on discovering cannabinoids from the cannabis plant. GW Pharmaceuticals' research is to discover uses of cannabinoids to treat cancer pain, diabetes, schizophrenia, glioma, epilepsy and much more. (fool.com)

## Revenue

Despite good news in 2018, GW Pharmaceuticals lost ground on this list for several reasons. The biggest reasons are regarding its stagnant share price and revenue. However, like many companies in this nascent industry, achieving financial success will be a marathon, not a sprint.

The success of GW Pharmaceuticals is largely tied to its primary product, cannabidiol (CBD) drug Epidiolex, which got FDA's approval earlier in 2018. So far, it currently has negative earnings. However, Goldman Sachs analyst Salveen Richter projects that epilepsy drug Epidiolex will eventually achieve over $2 billion annually. This can make GW's future market cap at almost $10 billion. GW has much potential if Epidiolex sales perform well commercially. (nasdaq.com)

## Epidiolex

In 2018, the Drug Enforcement Agency (DEA) awarded GW Pharmaceuticals, Epidiolex, Schedule V status, which is its least restrictive classification. Epidiolex is a liquid formulation of pure plant-derived cannabidiol. FDA gave GW Pharmaceuticals seven years to use Epidiolex for treatment of tuberous sclerosis complex (TSC), a disease known to cause many cases of epilepsy. Tests show success, with patients experiencing 39% fewer seizures than before.

Please note that despite DEA's Epidiolex decision, marijuana itself will remain for now a DEA Schedule I controlled substance—the highest restrictive classification. However, all told, we should rejoice that the DEA has finally recognized the potential health benefits of CBD. (gwpharm.com)

## Other Drugs

The firm also offers Sativex (nabiximols), which has been mostly used for the treatment of spasticity due to multiple sclerosis (MS). At the time of this writing, Sativex is not yet approved for sale in any form in the United States, since it failed an important phase 3 study on cancer pain. Regardless, Sativex has been approved for use in 30 other countries, including New Zealand and many territories in Europe. (forbes.com)

## Conclusion

The DEA and FDA has cleared the path for GW to begin marketing and selling the only CBD oil that's ever been cleared in the U.S. It also gives doctors the opportunity to potentially treat suffering patients who have epileptic episodes with something other than the long list of existing unsuccessful medications.

With a breakthrough product, plenty of cash on hand and nearly no debt, GW Pharmaceuticals is poised to improve on 2018, leading analysts to predict a rise in this marijuana stock's market value.

Visit gwpharm.com for more current information.

## Company Highlights (as of December 30, 2018)

Market Capitalization: $2.4 B

Shares Outstanding: 302.5 M

Revenue: $12.7 M

Industry: Pharmaceuticals

Share Price 52 Week Range: $7.07 - 15.00

# Company Profile

Address: Sovereign House, Cambridge, Cambridgeshire
CB24 9BZ

Phone: +44.1223.266800

Number of Employees: 583

Chief Executive Officer & Executive Director: Justin D.
Gover

Chief Operating Officer & Executive Director: Christopher
John Tovey

Chief Financial Officer: Scott M. Giacobello

Director-Clinical Operations: Richard Potts

# 7. OrganiGram Holdings Inc. (CVE:OGI) (OTCQB:OGRMF)

Like the licensed producers above, OrganiGram Holdings, Inc. also engages in the production and sale of medical marijuana in Canada. OrganiGram was founded on July 5, 2010 and is headquartered in Vancouver, Canada.

In this year's edition of our ebook, OrganiGram Holdings regained its footing after falling considerably down our list last year. If its recent earnings are any indication, Organigram has held up well since its product recall in 2016. The company's fast response to the recall and efficient management has satisfied most shareholders.

## Revenue

Organigram Holdings impressively announced a 131% increase in net sales of $12.4 million for the 2018 fiscal year versus $5.4 million in 2017. In addition, its sales for the fourth quarter increased a whopping 76% to $3.2 million versus last year's $1.8 million during the same time period.

The company also had a net income of $20.5 million in 2018, up almost 100% from 2017. Most of these gains came from the fourth quarter where Organigram clocked net income of $18 million versus a loss of $2 million for the same quarter last year. This was likely due to the legalization of recreational marijuana around that time.

"The importance of 2018 cannot be overstated for Organigram as well as the industry," said Greg Engel, the Company's Chief Executive Officer. "We are incredibly proud of our ability to meet the challenges of scaling our business in preparation for the adult recreational use market. We are pleased with our progress to date and believe that we have performed well in a highly competitive space while always maintaining a sustainable cost structure. Ultimately, it is our view that our Moncton Campus will be seen as a crown jewel in the industry as it is able to produce consistent, high-quality indoor grown product at scale to support our brands with the lowest dried flower cultivation costs reported to date in Canada."

Lastly, registered medical patients impressively increased to 15,730 in 2018 from 7,404 in 2017 or 112%. With Canada recently legalizing recreational marijuana, expect all these numbers to drastically improve in 2019. (organigram.ca)

## Certified Organic Product

Interestingly, what sets Organigram apart from other licensed producers is the fact they produce a certified organic product. With pot now essential considered a commodity (like wheat) in Canada, being certified organic differentiates Organigram's marijuana as a superior product with limited competition. In addition, since an organic producer is required to keep comprehensive records, this will appeal to doctors who will likely have more confidence prescribing an organic product to their patients.

## Expansion

In December 2018, Organigram announced it had secured a loan from Farm Credit Canada ("FCC") in the amount of $10M, which will be used to further finance their rapid expansion.

Currently, Organigram's production capacity is increasing with additional state-of-the-art grow rooms coming online in April 2019. This will increase the Company's target production capacity to over 150,000 kg per year.

Greg Engel, CEO of Organigram says, "The expansion of our facility represents the exceptional reputation of our team and products in the industry and among customers, and a focused strategic plan to ensure our continued global leadership. This increase in target production capacity further demonstrates Organigram's commitment and ability to support its partners and the growing demand across Canada for high quality adult recreational and medical products".

Organigram remains one of the top cannabis plays for investors. Visit organigram.ca for more current information.

## Company Highlights (as of December 2018)

Market Capitalization: $462.3 M

Shares Outstanding: 129.6 M

Price / Earnings: N/A

Revenue: $9.7 M

Net Profit Margin: 3.67%

Industry: Agricultural Commodities/ Milling

Share Price 52 Week Range: $2.57 - 6.68

## Company Profile

Address: 35A English Drive, Moncton, New Brunswick
E1E 3X3

Phone: +1.844.644.4726

Number of Employees: N/A

Chief Executive Officer: Greg Engel

Independent Director & Chief Operating Officer: Larry
Rogers

Chief Financial Officer: Paolo de Luca

## 8. Innovative Industrial Properties Inc. (NYSE: IIPR)

Innovative Industrial Properties Inc. was the first U.S. born company to be included on this list. It operates as an open-ended real estate investment trust (REIT).

### What is an REIT?

For those of you who do not know, a real estate investment trust is a company that owns and operates, income-producing real estate, ranging from apartment buildings to warehouses, hospitals, shopping centers and hotels. Stockholders of a REIT earn a large share of the income produced through the company's real estate investments. REITs are required to pay at least 90 percent of its taxable income in the form of shareholder dividends each year.

Innovative Industrial Properties is not as established as the other companies on this list, having just been added to NYSE late last year.

### On the NYSE

So why is it so high on this list? Besides an actual (current) dividend of 3.08%, the New York Stock Exchange made a rare move and allowed Industrial Properties to be included on their exchange. This was before Canadian producer, Tilray did the same thing later in 2018.

This was despite marijuana's illegal status on the federal level in the U.S. Therefore, if it is good enough for the NYSE, it's probably a safe bet among marijuana stocks.

Indeed, IIPR impressively increased its revenue in 2018, had its share price soar to new highs and has a highly experienced management team that has a proven track record of outperforming in the REIT space.

**Strategy**

As the company's home page says, "We target medical-use cannabis facilities for acquisition, including sale-leaseback transactions, with tenants that are licensed growers under long-term triple-net leases. We believe this industry is poised for significant growth in coming years, and we are focused on being a creative capital provider to this industry through the long-term ownership of cultivators' mission-critical facilities."

Their acquisition strategy is to act as a source of capital to licensed growers of medical marijuana by acquiring and leasing back their real estate locations. By leasing their properties back from IIPR, growers have the opportunity to redeploy the capital from the sale into their company's core operations.

## Acquisitions

In 2017, Innovative Industrial successfully acquired PharmaCannis property in New York. This created great revenue and the company got an impressive 17.2% cap rate. A few months later, IIPR entered a purchase agreement for a 72,000 square foot medical marijuana facility in Capitol Heights, Maryland. The building is still under construction and will be leased on a NNN basis to Holistic Industries LLC.

Like the PharmaCannis property, this Maryland property has three revenue streams for Innovative. This includes a base rent of 15% of the total amount IIPR invests-- higher than Pharmacannis' 12.7% of the purchase price. It will grow at 3.25% per year. IIPR will also collect a property management fee of 1.5% of base rent-- same as the Pharmacannis lease. Lastly, as rent reserve, IIPR will collect $1.9 per year from Holistic and $1.265 million per year for the first five years from Pharmacannis. (seekingalpha.com)

In July 2018, IIPR closed on the acquisition of a property located at 96 Palmer Road in Monson, Massachusetts for the purchase price of $12.75 million. This property is comprised of approximately 55,000 square feet of industrial space situated on approximately 5.4 acres. The acquisition is a long-term, triple-net lease agreement with Holistic Industries, Inc. This company will continue to operate the property as a medicinal cannabis cultivation and processing facility. (innovativeindustrialproperties.com)

Visit innovativeindustrialproperties.com/ for more current information.

## Company Highlights (as of December 30, 2018)

Market Capitalization: $443.7 M

Shares Outstanding: 9.8 M

52 Week Range: $23.63 - 55.63

Net Profit Margin: 38.85%

Revenue: $6.4 M

Industry: Real Estate Investment Trusts

Share Price 52 Week Range: $23.63 - 55.63

## Company Profile

Address: 11440 West Bernardo Court, San Diego, California 92127

Phone: 858-997-3332

Number of Employees: 6

Chief Executive Officer, President & Director: Paul Smithers

Executive Chairman: Alan Gold

Chief Financial Officer: Catherine Hastings

# 9. Auxly Cannabis Group Inc. (CVE: XLY) (OTCQX: CBWTF)

Auxly Cannabis Group, Inc. engages in investment, and financial and banking solutions. It focuses on equity and debt investments in private and public companies in various industries, especially the cannabis industry. Auxly specializes in all areas of the legal-cannabis supply chain, with a primary focus on upstream operations. This involves partnering with companies that grow the actual product. The company was founded on August 24, 1987 and is headquartered in Toronto, Canada.

## Cash-to-Debt Ratio

The biggest plus for Auxly is its favorable cash-to-debt ratio. With C$236.9 million in cash and cash equivalents at the end of the third quarter 2018, Auxly can make key acquisitions and investments while the marijuana market continues to grow. The company provides funding to the cannabis industry, which can be very difficult to get for early-stage companies, especially in the Unites States. In return for this funding, Auxly gets royalty payments and/or a stake in the company.

Auxly recently reported revenue of C$512,000, which is great compared to the zilch it made last year. With investments in more than 15 different marijuana-related businesses, Auxly has created a nicely diverse portfolio that minimizes risk for investors (investorplace.com)

## Expansion

Auxly recently announced a $15 million agreement to purchase an 80% stake in Inverell. Inverell is a company located in Uruguay, with aspirations to become the largest CBD producer in South America. As mentioned in the last chapter, the South American market is growing leaps and bounds, yet is still virtually untapped.

Auxly also has an agreement with Dixie Brands, which is the parent company of Dixie Elixir, a leading producer of cannabinoid-infused products. The agreement includes the exclusive right to produce and distribute Dixie products across Canada.

Despite these developments, the company has accrued a lot of costs in marketing and in its expansion efforts. Management was even forced to issue more shares. As long-term investors know all too well, this stock is a great opportunity. Future share prices will reflect this.

Visit auxly.com for more current information.

# Company Highlights (as of December 30, 2018)

Market Capitalization: $388.3 M

Shares Outstanding: 584.8 M

52 Week Range: $0.44 - 2.70

Revenue: C$512,000

Industry: Investment Banks/Brokers

Share Price 52 Week Range: $0.44 - 2.70

# Company Profile

Address: 777 Richmond Street West, Toronto, Ontario M6J 0C2

Phone: +1.647.812.0121

Number of Employees: N/A

Chief Executive Officer: Chuck Charles Rifici

President & Director: Hugo M. Alves

Chief Financial Officer: Jeff Tung

# 10. Marimed Inc. (OTCMKTS:MRMD).

The American-based MariMed, Inc. engages in the development and management of compliant facilities for the cultivation, production, and dispensing of legal cannabis and cannabis-infused products. It also provides its clients legal, accounting, human resources, and other corporate and administrative services.

It operates through the Online Portal Operations and Cannabis Operations. The Online Portal Operations segment owns a proprietary technology platform, select URLs, and a vast inventory of digital assets. The company was founded by Robert Fireman and Jon Levine on January 25, 2011 and is headquartered in Newton, MA.

## Revenue

In June, Marimed reported $2.9 million in revenue, which is an increase of 81% from the same period in 2017. Despite the company's terrific trajectory year over year, it also realized a net loss of approximately 8 million. The is mostly due to issuance of stock options and warrants, and the settlements of debt. Excluding these non-cash items, net income for Marimed for the three and six months ended June 30, 2018 was approximately $575,000 and $530,000, respectively.

Lastly, both cash in hand and assets tripled in size. Management at MariMed is confident that the company

will grow to $100 million in annual revenue.
(marimedadvisors.com)


## Expansion

According to MariMed, the company manages facilities in
New Bedford and Middleborough, Massachusetts; Anna
and Harrisburg, Illinois; Wilmington and Lewes, Delaware;
Hagerstown, Maryland; and Clark, Nevada. Hagerstown is
the biggest facility covering 100,000 square feet of
marijuana production space. The total value of all these
facilities is in excess of $30 million.
(marimedadvisors.com)


## Conclusion

Interestingly, when investors were collecting profits and
stocks prices fell in October, Marimed stock stayed tough
with share prices actually climbing almost 19%. Compared
to other stocks in this list, analysts generally agree that
Marimed has loads of potential in 2019.


Visit marimedadvisors.com for more current information.

## Company Highlights (as of December 30, 2018)

Market Capitalization: $691.6 M

Shares Outstanding: 212.8 M

52 Week Range: $0.52 - 5.80

Revenue: $6.1 M

Industry: Packaged Software

Share Price 52 Week Range: $0.52 - 5.80

## Company Profile

Address: 26 Ossipee Road, Newton, Massachusetts 02464

Phone: +1.844.244.0200

Number of Employees: 12

Chief Executive Officer: Robert N. Fireman

Chief Operating Officer: Tim Shaw

Chief Financial Officer: Jon Levine

# 11. Terra Tech Corporation (OTC:TRTC)

A favorite small cap stock in the United States, Terra Tech Corp. is a vertically integrated cannabis-focused agriculture company, which engages in cultivating and providing medical cannabis. Because production is vertically integrated, the company is involved in growing and processing the raw plant material, as well as selling the end product.

Founded in 2008 and headquartered in Newport Beach, CA, Terra Tech Corp is "pioneering the future by integrating the best of the natural world with technology to create sustainable solutions for medical cannabis production, extraction and distribution, plant science research and development, food production and Closed Environment Agriculture (CEA). Through this development, we have created relevant brands in both the cannabis and agriculture industries." (terratechcorp.com)

## Multiple Subsidiaries

Terra Tech Corp. operates through multiple subsidiary businesses including: Blüm, IVXX Inc., Edible Garden, MediFarm LLC and GrowOp Technology. Through these subsidiaries, TRTC is committed to cultivating and providing the high quality medical cannabis consistently delivered to qualified, registered medical marijuana establishments.

Terra Tech's subsidiary, Blüm offers a broad selection of medical marijuana products including flowers and edibles throughout its California and Nevada locations. Subsidiary, IVXX, Inc. produces medical cannabis-extracted products for regulated medical cannabis dispensaries throughout California. The wholly-owned subsidiary, Edible Garden, cultivates a premier brand of local and sustainably grown hydroponic produce, sold through major grocery stores such as ShopRite, Walmart, Kroger, and others throughout the East coast and the Midwest. MediFarm LLC is focused on medical cannabis cultivation and permitting businesses throughout Nevada. Lastly, the wholly-owned subsidiary GrowOp Technology, specializes in controlled environment agricultural technologies. (terratechcorp.com)

## Revenue

Terra Tech has seen tremendous growth in 2018. Unfortunately, it has also seen net income losses as well, mainly due to its expansion projects. After hitting all times highs in share price, Terra Tech Corp found selling pressure on reporting disappointing Q3 financial results. Revenues in the quarter slumped to $7.1 million from $10.1 million reported last year.

The company reported most of the fall in revenue is due to its subsidiary IVXX, when its production facilities were relocated. It proved to be very costly, but the company expects the expense will be worth it, since the much improved facility will facilitate increased and efficient production.

"We invested in our organic growth by working toward upgrading our IVXX® production facilities to optimize efficiency and output at our wholesale business. While this transition impacted revenues in the short term, these steps will allow us to increase production and achieve greater distribution throughout California, building a more defensible and scalable long-term business model," said Chief executive Officer Derek Peterson. (terratechcorp.com)

**Expansion**

In the beginning of 2018, California officially became an enormous market for recreational marijuana. TRTC's value consequently surged even more than it did when Nevada legalized earlier in 2017. Of all the marijuana penny stocks, Terra Tech is set to benefit the most from legalization in California.

In addition to pursuing growth opportunities domestically, Terra Tech is also focused on international expansion. The management yearns to make the company a market leader, like the other companies ahead on this list. As part of its expansion goals, Terra Tech is looking for merger and acquisition opportunities.

In 2018, Terra Tech signed a binding letter to merge with Golden Leaf Holdings. The merger will allow Terra Tech to expand and increase its stronghold over California, Oregon and Nevada, with 41 permits.

Analysts expect Terra Tech's expansion to increase revenue considerably in 2019. (seekingalpha.com)

Visit terratechcorp.com for more current information.

## Company Highlights (as of December 30, 2018)

Market Capitalization: $45.6 M

Shares Outstanding: 80.7 M

Revenue: $35.8 M

Industry: Agricultural Commodities/Milling

Share Price 52 Week Range: $0.46 - 9.38

## Company Profile

Address: 2040 Main Street, Irvine, California 92614

Phone: +1.855.447.6967

Number of Employees: 270

Chairman, President & Chief Executive Officer: Derek A. Peterson

Chief Operating Officer & Director: Michael A. Nahass

Chief Financial Officer & Accounting Officer: Michael C. James

# 12. mCig Inc. (OTC: MCIG)

Another favorite penny stock in the United States is mCig Incorporated. mCIg is another fast-growing company, whose earnings reports keep growing at an outstanding pace. Headquartered in Beverly Hills and founded in 2010, the company operates through two divisions: mCig Construction and mCig Commercial.

The mCig Construction division develops, designs and constructs modular buildings with unique and proprietary elements that assist cannabis growers in the market. This full-service construction company currently operates in the Nevada market, but plans to expand once federal laws change.

The mCig Commercial division manufactures, distributes, and retails the mCig - an affordable loose-leaf eCig, which apparently provides a smoother inhalation experience. It offers electronic cigarettes and related products through its online store mcig.org, as well as through the company's wholesale, distributor, and retail programs. (mcig.org)

## Revenue

The company has successfully expanded from generating e-cigarettes to various avenues for growth in the cannabis industry. Revenue for mCig almost doubled year over year to $7.1 million.

However, mCig's share price performance has not been as great in 2018 as it was in 2017. In 2017, mCig gained 104.1% whereas the S&P 500 gained 19.4%. In 2018 year to date (December), mCig fell about 55% vs. a loss of about 8% for the S&P 500. This is more to do with the fact that the market in general is retracting, and penny stocks retract the most. See our chapter on strategies to understand how small stocks have more volatility.

**Supply Division Expands Operations in California**

By the beginning of 2018, mCig reported that its supply segment, Cannabiz Supply had expanded its operations into California. Cannabiz introduced its operation in Temecula, California capitalizing on months of groundwork and will begin creating revenue ahead of its estimated implementation plan. The segment will be working with dispensaries and production facilities in fulfilling their supply needs for businesses throughout the vast California region, where recreational marijuana has been fully legalized.

Visit www.mcig.org for more current information.

## Company Highlights (as of December 30, 2018)

Market Capitalization: $77.5 M

Shares Outstanding: 517.0 M

Revenue: $7.1 M

Industry: Industrial Machinery

Share Price 52 Week Range: $0.14 - 0.43


## Company Profile

Address: 4720 Salisbury Road, Jacksonville, Florida 32256

Phone: +1.570.778.6459

Number of Employees: 73

Chairman, President & Chief Executive Officer: Paul Rosenberg

Chief Financial Officer: Michael Hawkins

Chief Technology Officer: Patrick Lucey

Chief Research & Development Officer: Michael Snody

# 13. Auscann Holdings (ASX:AC8) (OTC:ACNNF)

In 2018, Auscann Group Holdings was added to the Australian index ASX after completing a successful reverse takeover of TW Holdings. AusCann is well positioned to take advantage of the developing medical marijuana market because of its strong team. The team includes the experienced, Canadian pot producer, Canopy Growth Corporation (TSE:WEED) and Chilean medicinal cannabis grower Fundación Daya. Since its addition to the ASX, Auscann's stock price has more than quadrupled.

## Canopy Growth Corp Partnership

Canopy supplies AusCann with knowledge and experience, not to mention product as AusCann's first harvest prepares for sale. In addition, Chile's Daya was the first company in Chile legally allowed to grow medical marijuana. With its team and management in place, AusCann imports cannabis products from Canopy Growth to meet the demand of Chile and Australia's many consumers. When combined, Chile and Australia's population is about equal to the population of Canada! (https://www.businessinsider.com)

**Revenue Potential**

The Auscann Group's share price is down substantially since hitting a high of $1.85 in early 2018, when the federal government announced it would permit the export from Australia of medicinal marijuana.

Despite the young company still not delivering revenue, it reached a market cap north of $270 million for much of early 2018, showing how much potential investors see in this company.

In late October, Auscann claims it is "aiming to release its first capsule-based pharmaceuticals for clinical trials and patients in the first half of 2019". (auscann.com.au)

Visit http://www.auscann.com.au/ for more information.

## Company Highlights (as of December 30, 2018)

Market Capitalization: $68.8 M

Shares Outstanding: 176.4 M

Revenue: N/A

Price / Earnings: 21.33

Industry: Biotech & Pharma

Share Price 52 Week Range: $0.32 - 1.75

## Company Profile

Address: 2831 St. Rose Parkway, Henderson, Nevada 89052

Phone: +1.571.426.0107

Number of Employees: N/A

Chairman: Dr. Mal Washer

Managing Director: Elaine Darby

Executive Director: Harry Karelis

# 14. Medical Marijuana, Inc. (OTC: MJNA)

Another U.S. penny stock with amazing potential, Medical Marijuana Inc. engages in the provision of various business management solutions to the hemp and medical marijuana industries. It is comprised of a diversified portfolio of products, services, technology and businesses solely focused on the cannabis and hemp industries. The company was founded in 2003 and is headquartered in Poway, CA.

With a current market cap value of $221.5M, MJNA has a reserve of $755K of cash on the books, which compares with about $808K in total current liabilities. MJNA is seeing major top-line growth, with y/y quarterly revenues growing at 230.5%.

## Latin American Influence

With the approval of MJNA's product Real Scientific Hemp Oil, Brazil became the first Latin American country to approve prescriptions for a medical cannabis product. In addition, a THC-free version of this Hemp Oil was also the first medical cannabis product accepted into Mexico when it was approved as a prescription medication early in 2016. It was authorized for a young girl Grace, who suffered up to 400 seizures a day. Although Mexico had approved the use of CBD for patients with a doctor's prescription, the government remained opposed to products with even trace amounts of THC in them. In order to import their CBD hemp oil to Mexico, MJNA had to develop a product

completely free of THC and it succeeded.
(medicalmarijuanainc.com)

Later in 2017, HempMeds Mexico opened its first office in Mexico. The announcement received international media attention during the July 28, 2017 inauguration of the office in Monterrey, Nuevo Leon, Mexico. Medical Marijuana, Inc. CEO Dr. Stuart Titus stated, "We appreciate the outpouring of support that we received at the opening of the first HempMeds® Mexico office in Monterrey, Mexico, which reflects a growing demand for the Company's zero-Tetrahidrocannabidiol (THC) Real Scientific Hemp Oil-X™ (RSHO-X™). The extensive coverage that we received from both local and international media is a testament to the worldwide interest in cannabis reform happening in Mexico, and the efforts of HempMeds® Mexico to provide products for this rapidly expanding CBD hemp oil market."

In May 2016, Real Scientific Hemp Oil became the first medical cannabis product approved and imported for use in Paraguay. This event marked the third time in a little over a year that RSHO was the first cannabis product approved in a Latin American country.

HempMeds Brazil also gained media attention in Brazilian newspapers after a Federal judge there ordered the government to subsidize payments for Real Scientific Hemp Oil for a Brazilian citizen.

## Revenue

In August 2018, Medical Marijuana, Inc announced that the company and its subsidiaries have booked their grandest sales revenue quarter in their history. In addition, they reached important milestones in their various international operations.

MJNA's Q2 2018 revenues exceeded $14.8 million, an increase of more than 40% year over year. In addition, the total gross profits for Q2 2018 more than doubled.

The list of MJNA's accomplishments in 2018 are long. They include launching its very first "CBD vape cartridge through subsidiary Dixie Botanicals, experiencing three consecutive record-breaking sales months and announcing a partnership with Peak Health to distribute the first-ever, and only, hops (Kriya brand Humulus)-derived CBD extract, ImmunAg." (prnewswire.com)

"In Q2 we saw significant media coverage and operational successes," said Medical Marijuana, Inc. CEO Dr. Stuart Titus. "As we move into Q3, we will aim to continuously make our mark in the cannabis space with our portfolio of high-quality cannabis products, all while increasing shareholder value."

## Invite to United Nations

MJNA made headlines when CFN Media Group discussed the company's invite to the United Nations.

CEO Dr. Stuart Titus stated, "We are honored and excited to speak to United Nations leaders on a global stage about CBD as a supplement aimed to maintain and improve the wellbeing of millions. We hope to bring light to the many benefits of CBD and convince decision-makers that CBD in its natural botanical state, derived from hemp, should be classified as a supplement."

## Company of Firsts

Medical Marijuana, Inc. bills itself as a company of firsts. After all, it was the first publicly traded cannabis company in the United States in 2010. MJNA is also the first U.S. marijuana company to establish a global pipeline to other countries, especially Mexico, Brazil and Paraguay. According to their website, MJNA was also the first to introduce cannabis foods and supplements across U.S. state lines and international borders.

To see their other firsts, visit
http://www.medicalmarijuanainc.com/

# Company Highlights (as of December 30, 2018)

Market Capitalization: $266.4 M

Shares Outstanding: 3.2 B

Revenue: $26.5 M

Industry: Biotech/ Pharma

Share Price 52 Week Range: $0.06 - 0.19

## Company Profile

Address: 13831 Danielson, Poway, California 92064

Phone: +1.866.273.8502

Number of Employees: 85

Chairman, President, Chief Executive Officer & CFO: Stuart W. Titus

Chief Operating Officer & Executive Vice President: Blake N. Schroeder

International Vice President: Alex Grapov

Vice President-Business Development: Nick Massalas

# 15. Maricann Group Inc. (CNSX: MARI) (OTC: MRRCF)

Maricann Group, Inc. is a producer and distributor of medical cannabis. The company operates a cultivation, marijuana extraction and distribution business under federal license from the Government of Canada. Its products include Bubba Kush, Icann Oil, Forte 190, and MK Ultra. The company was founded in 2013 and is headquartered in Burlington, Canada.

## Revenue

Maricann is quietly increasing their revenue year over year, making their long-term investors proud. By mid 2018, Maricann reported revenue of a little over $1 million and $1.7 million for the three and six months ended June 30, 2018, respectively. This is compared to $661,602 and $1,804,769 during the same periods a year ago.

"We have achieved significant supply agreements with a number of provinces to supply our cannabis products which is expected to transform into shareholder value with compelling revenue in Q4 2018, 2019 and beyond. As previously disclosed, the Company has reserved product for the recreational market commencing October 17th and its pharmacy joint initiative commencing October 1st. The Company made the conscious decision to preserve inventory to meet demand for these strategic long-term sales channels, said Ben Ward CEO of Maricann. (maricann.com)

## Maricann's Aggressive Expansion

Despite its share price down-trending as of late, Maricann Group Inc is a $150 million company gaining a foothold in international markets. Its strong expansion strategy includes a venture into Germany's large marijuana market. This started with a $42.5 million acquisition of 150,000 square feet of cultivation operations in a Ebersbach facility, as well as 250,000 square feet expansion of their two-tiered cultivation plan and outdoor hemp farm. Considering these acquisitions were made at a discount, they provided the company with a boost in asset valuation.

Maricann's CEO, Benjamin Ward states, "The Ebersbach facility offers Maricann a significant advantage in cost of overall construction and speed to market…. To construct a similar facility today, the estimated cost would be over 120 million EUR. Maricann entered into a reservation agreement to purchase the facility for a total price of 3,410,000 EUR at closing." (newcannabisventures.com)

## Conclusion

Despite its early growing pains, Maricann has positioned itself as a global player, investing heavily in its bid to expand internationally. Analysts expect this company to be extremely profitable as the world continues to accept marijuana as a viable commodity, especially its home Canada where recreational marijuana just became legal.

For more information, visit maricann.com.

## Company Highlights (as of December 30, 2018)

Market Capitalization: $142.0 M

Shares Outstanding: 212.0 M

Revenue: $2.5 M

Industry: Pharmaceuticals

Share Price 52 Week Range: $0.65 - 3.60

## Company Profile

Address: 845 Harrington Court, Burlington, Ontario L7N 3P3

Phone: +1.289.288.6274

Number of Employees: N/A

Chief Operating Officer: James Hyssen

Chief Executive Officer & Director: Ben Ward

President: Terry Fretz

# 16. VIVO Cannabis Inc (TSX-V: VIVO) (VVCIF:OTCQX)

Formerly ABcann Medicinals, VIVO is headquared in Canada, and is a cost efficient producer of quality, organically grown, standardized plant based medicines. Though currently low on our list, VIVO rose fast in 2018 to be an international leader in the cannabis market. Subsidiary, ABcann Medicinals Inc. was one of the first companies to obtain a production license under the Marijuana for Medical Purposes Regulations.

## Organic Marijuana

VIVO's flagship facility in Napanee, Ontario uses cutting-edge plant-growing technology to consistently produce organically grown and pesticide-free plants. In turn, these plants generate high-quality cannabis products. In 2018, VIVO expanded capacity to approximately 30,000 square feet. At the same time, VIVO opened a new 150,000 square foot facility in Napanee. (vivocannabis.com)

## Product Line

By the beginning of 2018, VIVO announced the release of a product with a high, yet legal CBD:THC (cannabidol:tetrahydrocannabinol) ratio. This is part of the company's strategy to provide a diverse range of products as it begins to sell cannabis oils to its customers. This product CBD-Med has a ratio of 27.6:1 (18.5% CBD to 0.67% THC). This is one of Canada's highest CBD products under Health Canada regulations.

VIVO has made available to patients a 1-1 THC/CBD drop, a high THC dropper and a high CBD dropper. This is in addition to ABcann's current high CBD products: NC:Med - 18.9:1 (18.9% CBD to 1% THC) and DC:Med - 15.4:1 (15.4% CBD to 1% THC). Expect capsule products and soft gels to arrive shortly.

"The development of these products is in line with ABcann's corporate strategy as a premium product provider of organic, pesticide free cannabis," says Ken Clement, Executive Chairman of VIVO. "As the Company continues to scale production capacity, our product line will expand as we strive to increase shareholder value through capturing a larger market share of the current global medical markets." (Globe Newswire)

### Revenue

In late 2018, VIVO made investors very happy when they announced their latest financial results. The results are the company's best financial performance to date.

"The acquisition of Canna Farms represents a transformational transaction in the evolution of VIVO that has led to a record quarter of $2.3 million revenue, with

$4.4 million of pro forma revenue for the full quarter. Not only has this acquisition provided a significant revenue impact, it has tripled our production capacity, expanded our product range and substantially increased our medical patient base," stated Barry Fishman, CEO of VIVO.

With a revenue of $2.3 million, VIVO also reported a net loss of $9.1 million for the third quarter of 2018, a result of its costs in investing for future growth in the wake of Canada's launch of the recreational marijuana market on October 17, 2018.

As of September 2018, VIVO had $100 million in cash, total assets of $285 million, liabilities of $61 million, and 291 million common shares outstanding.

**Expansion**

VIVO Cannabis impressively achieved a lot in regards to its bid for expansion. In August 2018, VIVO completed the acquisition of Canna Farms, resulting in Q3 revenue of $4.4 M. VIVO also entered into supply agreements with British Columbia, Alberta, Saskatchewan, Manitoba, Ontario and the Yukon. They also introduced their recently launched Beacon Medical™ product into Australian markets.

By the end of third quarter, VIVO also had a total of 18,000 medical marijuana patients, compared to the 2,000 patients they had only one quarter ago. (vivocannabis.com)

For more up-to-date information, visit vivocannabis.com.

## Company Highlights (as of December 30, 2018)

Market Capitalization: $75.6 M

Shares Outstanding: 291.0 M

Revenue: $150.1 M

Industry: Agriculture

Share Price 52 Week Range: $0.41 - 3.29

## Company Profile

Address: 126 Vanluven Road, Napanee, Ontario K7R 3L2

Phone: +1.613.232.1567

Number of Employees: N/A

Chief Executive Office: Barry Fisherman

Chief Financial Officer: Michael Bumby

Vice President & GM-Napanee Operations: Jenny Guan

# 17. Medmen Enterprises (CNSX: MMEN) (OTCQX: MMNFF)

MedMen Enterprises, Inc. engages in the cultivation, production, and retailing of cannabis supply chain. It is a U.S.-based cannabis company with operations in California, Nevada, New York, and Florida. MedMen owns and operates 19 licensed cannabis facilities in cultivation, manufacturing, and retail. Its facilities use agronomic technology and sustainable techniques. The company was founded by Adam Bierman and Andrew Modlin on January 9, 2018 and is headquartered in Culver City, CA.

## Revenue

It was no coincidence why Marijuana retail outfit MedMen Enterprises suddenly became an investor favorite in mid-October, when it surged over 60% at its peak. Highlights of 2018 include annual and fourth quarter revenues of $39.8 million and $20.6 million, respectively.

What sets MedMen from most companies on our list is the fact that it is a vertically integrated organization. Its operations include production, extraction, branding and distribution. This enables Medmen to virtually control its own supply chain. As Medmen CEO Adam Bierman stated recently, this structure lets MedMen lower costs, enabling better profit margins within its immediate future. (medmen.com)

## Expansion

MedMen will enter 2019 with a leading US market position with 12 states, 67 retail stores and 14 factories with pending PharmaCann acquisition. In 2018, MedMen added 8 store locations throughout California, New York and Nevada, with signed agreements to enter Arizona and Illinois markets soon.

"Since becoming a public company in May of this year (2018), we've been singularly focused on our vision to mainstream marijuana and I'm proud to say that our hard work and the significant investments we've made in building our operating platform and team are paying off. For fiscal 2018, we delivered solid revenues of almost $40 million and over half of that was in the fourth quarter alone, indicative of the strong momentum in our business and our growth potential," said Adam Bierman, MedMen's chief executive officer and co-founder. "2018 is a year of many milestones, including the pending PharmaCann acquisition; closed and pending expansions to Northern California, Illinois, Arizona and Florida; successes in accessing the capital markets; and the launch of our suite of [statemade] products and brand strategy. With our strengthened Board of Directors and management team, diverse asset base and strong balance sheet, we believe we are well positioned to capture the future potential of the evolving cannabis industry."

Other developments include acquiring the assets of Nevada Wellness Project, LLC, in June 2018, opening a new store on Venice's trendy Abbot Kinney Blvd, opening Project Mustang-- a state-of-the-art cultivation and production facility in Reno, Nevada, acquiring San Diego Health and Wellness Center's assets, including a dispensary license; and lastly acquiring two more dispensary licenses in Nevada. (Nasdaq.com)

For more up-to-date information, visit medmen.com.

## Company Highlights (as of December 30, 2018)

Market Capitalization: $81.1 M

Shares Outstanding: 28.8 M

Revenue: $39.8 M

Industry: Pharmaceuticals

Share Price 52 Week Range: $2.53 - 7.57

## Company Profile

Address: 10115 Jefferson Boulevard, Culver City, California 90232

Phone: +1.855.292.8399

Number of Employees: 800

Chief Executive Officer & Director: Adam Bierman

President & Director: Andrew Modlin

Chief Financial Officer: Michael W. Kramer

# 18. Aleafia Health Inc. (TSX: ALEF) (ALEAF:OTCQX)

Aleafia's unique patient-focused, healthcare solution and its substantial cultivation, research and clinical assets have created one of Canada's leading, vertically integrated medical cannabis companies.

Aleafia Health, Inc. provides healthcare services, which focuses on medical cannabis solutions. The company operates medical cannabis care through nation-wide medical cannabis clinics, a world-class processing and distribution facility, and innovative research. Aleafia Health is headquartered in Concord, Canada.

## Revenue

Highlights of 2018 include a total revenue for the last quarter that went up 36 per cent over the previous quarter. Gross profit escalated in favorable fashion as well.

With Aleafia's Farms & Products division, Q3 2018 revenue and operating income before non-cash items was $529,146 and $217,358, respectively. This includes the young company's first harvest sale. By the end of 2018, the Company had over $20 million in cash on hand.

Aleafia also started a cannabis division with Serruya Private Equity that includes a $10 million strategic investment in Aleafia.

"As the company has achieved a number of important milestones, we are extremely encouraged by our third quarter results. It has been a transformative period for Aleafia. Our first cannabis sale marks the beginning of our cultivation expansion with Aleafia producing 98,000 kg of dried flower on an annual run rate basis," said Aleafia Chairman Julian Fantino. "We look forward to soon supplying our growing base of over 50,000 patients with Aleafia-produced medical cannabis." (aleafiainc.com)

## Expansion

Aleafia aggressively expanded in 2018. Their achievements include the retrofitting of a 160,000 Sq. Ft. Niagara Greenhouse that will greatly lessen operating costs and allow higher profit margins. This facility's first harvest is predicted for spring 2019.

Aleafia is also expecting its new acquisition-- a 60,000 kg, secure outdoor cannabis cultivation site at Aleafia's Health Canada-Licensed Port Perry facility will break ground in the Spring of 2019, with its first harvest expected for the following summer. (aleafiainc.com)

For more up-to-date information, visit aleafiainc.com.

## Company Highlights (as of December 30, 2018)

Market Capitalization: $165.5 M

Shares Outstanding: 157.6 M

Revenue: $3.0 M

Industry: Medical/Nursing Services

Share Price 52 Week Range: $0.37 - 3.62


## Company Profile

Address: 8810 Jane Street, Concord, Ontario L4K 2M9

Phone: +1.416.860.5665

Number of Employees: N/A

Chief Executive Officer: Geoffrey M. Benic

Chief Marketing & Technology Officer: Trevor James Newell

Chief Financial Officer: Benjamin Ferdinand

# Marijuana IPOs of 2019: The Future Hot Stocks

No doubt 2018 was a phenomenal year for marijuana-related enterprises. Not only did Canada fully legalize recreation marijuana, but other countries took giant leaps into the market as well. Even conservative states in America like Utah and Oklahoma realized how much their population demanded the benefits of cannabis. The population of California alone dwarfs that of every other legal market combined. 2019 is shaping up to be an even better year. Investors and companies fully understand how a nascent industry such as this one could blossom as the world continues to tip its scales into its favor.

The next round of initial public offerings (IPOs) in the marijuana sector will mostly come from U.S.-based companies looking to expand their bottom lines—despite the fact that cannabis remains illegal under federal law. There's already a myriad of Canadian companies vying for top spots in its newly created recreational cannabis market. Canadian companies like Tilray Inc (TLRY) now have to deliver on their promises after they IPO'ed in 2018.

Without further adieu, here are several companies that will likely go public in 2019:

## 1.) Dr. Kerklaan Therapeutics

Dr. Kerklaan Therapeutics is a California-based manufacturer of CBD-infused topical creams and sprays that help alleviate pain and inflammation. Their revenue has increased 100% on a monthly basis since mid-2018. Expect it to continue beyond $10 million next year. According to the company's president, Andrew Kerklaan, they plan to file for an IPO in 2019.

For more up-to-date information, visit https://drkerklaan.com/.

## 2.) Pax Labs

This San Francisco-based vaporizer company raised $20 million from investors in October for its marijuana-related products—like its portable loose-leaf Vaporizer. These investors include Altria Group Inc (MO). This puts the company at a valuation of $5 billion. Pax is hoping since it does not directly work with or touch marijuana, a major exchange like NASDAQ will permit it to be listed.

For more up-to-date information, visit https://www.paxvapor.com/.

### 3.) Harborside

Also known as FLRish IP, Harborside was formerly a nonprofit medical marijuana dispensary. Now it is eagerly trying to become a for-profit business listed on the CSE in early 2019. According to CEO Andrew Berman, Harborside wants to raise about $50 million. To achieve this goal, Berman hopes the company will complete a reverse takeover of an already listed company. Its expansion goals include additional retail operations in California.

For more up-to-date information, visit https://www.shopharborside.com/.


### 4.) Cannalife Capital Corp.

Based in Vancouver, Canada, Cannalife's expertise is in acquiring marijuana-related brands. In October 2018, the company closed on 5 new portfolio investments.

From New York to California, there are several blossoming markets in the U.S and Cannalife is making the most of it. In 2019, they will continue to target and make investments in these brands that have leverage to these markets.

For more up-to-date information, visit http://cannalifecapital.com/.

### 5.) Raw Garden

Another California company based in the Santa Barbara region, Raw Garden is a top marijuana-concentrate company, specializing in cannabis oil. According to experts, Raw Garden continues to impress with ever-increasing revenue and low costs in its operation, despite its aggressive expansion endeavors. Their planned IPO in 2019 will do wonders for their ambitious plans.

For more up-to-date information, visit https://rawgarden.farm/.

### 6.) Magical Butter

With a name like Magical Butter, it's hard to imagine this Florida-based company won't continue its impressive success into 2019. Founded in 2012, the company sells blenders for customers to create their own cannabis butters and infusions. The company reported surging revenue last year and plans to start trading on the Canadian stock exchange in early 2019. Magical Butter has an arsenal of strategic relationships with many major marijuana companies.

For more up-to-date information, visit https://magicalbutter.com/.

### 7.) PharmaCielo

PharmaCielo is a cultivator in Columbia, which is often sited as one of the best places in the world to grow cannabis due to its perfect climate conditions and its cheap energy costs. PharmaCielo has 15 million square feet of production facilities, plus owns Colombia's only e-clinic platform with 80,000 registered patients.

As its official website says, "The PharmaCielo team is committed to fostering the world's leading supplier of naturally grown and processed, standardized medicinal-grade cannabis oil extracts and related products."

For more up-to-date information, visit https://www.pharmacielo.com/.


### 8.) InterCure Ltd.

Headquartered in Israel and founded in 1994, InterCure Ltd. intends to have their company go public in 2019, on the major exchange Nasdaq. Like many companies on this list, the company mostly cultivates cannabis at various facilities, located in Israel and Europe.

For more up-to-date information, visit https://www.crunchbase.com/organization/intercure-inc.

# Researching Companies

The companies listed in the last chapter all have great potential to be profitable investments for you. As these companies mature, keep studying their metrics to determine if they remain worth holding. Furthermore, since performance can change in time, you may have to consider companies beyond this list. And you should. After all, every month there are more publicly traded cannabis companies added to exchanges around the world.

In the ever-changing landscape of the stock market, it's important for investors to learn how to appropriately choose a stock to invest in. The waters get murkier when the pool of stocks you are checking out are growth stocks. This is because growth stocks will more often than not use their capital for expansion projects, which will result in their fundamentals showing debt and negative cash flow.

Below are tips on how to evaluate and research growth stocks in this sector or any other sector. When studying these guidelines, it helps to look beyond numbers and remind yourself you are buying a piece of this company. Therefore, wouldn't you like to be as educated as possible on everything there is to know about the company?

Also keep in mind, even if the company is not in your country, we live in an age where the internet can provide nearly all the information you need. Even the smallest of companies has plenty of information online if you dig enough.

# Study Outstanding Shares

A key metric that is often overlooked is the number of shares outstanding. **Outstanding shares** refer to a company's stock currently held by all its shareholders. For instance, a typical new trader might view Company X as more valuable than Company Y, simply because X has a higher share price. Let's assume they have the same market cap of $100M too. Now, when you consider each company's outstanding shares, you would observe company X has 1 billion outstanding shares, in comparison to company Y, which has only 1 million outstanding shares.

Sometimes through a secondary offering or share issuance to raise capital, a company might dilute its shares. This means the number of shares outstanding can often balloon out of control. Through stock splits or through secondary offerings, it often dilutes the ownership percentage held by holding investors. The trade-off, though, is that the company gets to keep the cash raised, which increases its overall value.

When a company whose stock you own dilutes its shares, your first move should be to figure out whether you think the price the company will get for its shares reflects its fair value. If the company is getting a good deal, then that's positive. If not, you may want to lessen or close your position. Another possibility is that an insider is selling their large position, which might suggest a bad sign too.

Share issuance isn't necessarily bad, but they do require due diligence. Understanding the motivation behind them is important in order to make the right move.

## Revenue Growth

Revenue growth alone is often not the best metric for growth stocks. While studying the average revenue growth of a company for the previous few years can be helpful, an investor should also look at the potential profitability of the company. To do this, an investor should study the company's losses, debt, financing, efficient use of capital, brand recognition, etc.

# Financing

A company closing a round of financing at around current stock prices is positive news. After all, the more capital raised, the greater the odds of success-- especially if the investors themselves are reputable. For instance, Canadian unicorn, Canopy Growth Corp. owns a considerable amount of newbie AusCann Holdings. This shows investors around the world that AusCann is a legit company.

Even though financing is usually a positive sign, it can be negative as well. For instance, if a company closes a financing deal at a 70% discount to market price, it's almost certain they are desperate for money. Therefore, when you do your due diligence, establish what price the financing took place. If a company raises money at too great of a discount to the current stock price, it's also a sign the current price is probably overvalued.

# Profitability

In order to grow, a growth stock needs capital. Besides borrowing money, most capital comes from profits. In order for these companies to expand, they need to sometimes spend quite a bit. It's because of this that these companies will not be offering dividends any time soon.

**Earnings Per Share**

A great metric to understand a company's profitability is earnings per share (EPS). EPS shows how a company's profits are allocated to each share. This will reveal the per-share allocation of a company's profits.

EPS is used in calculating price/earnings ratio (P/E). Keep in mind, while an established company might have a P/E of around 25, a growth stock will often have a much higher P/E since its funds are often used for expansion and keeping the lights on.

### Operating Margin and Net Margin

Two popular metrics for researching growth stocks are operating margin and net margin.

**Operating margin** is a measurement of what percentage of a company's revenue is left over after paying for variable costs of production such as raw materials, and wages. Consequently, it becomes a great measure of a company's management, since it reveals how they are controlling operating costs.

**Net margin** is the percentage of revenue remaining after all operating expenses have been deducted from a company's total revenue. These expenses include interest and taxes.

Both metrics are especially useful when compared to industry and competitor's averages. Furthermore, an investor should consider how these measures are trending over previous years. Strong growth in these numbers show financial stability and extra working capital.

## Efficient Use of Capital

Investors also need to examine how a company uses its capital for the company's best interests, like market share or new products. Two excellent metrics are ROA (return on assets) and ROE (return on equity). Both numbers are designed to show how effectively a company utilizes its current assets to generate additional profits.

## ROA

Displayed as a percentage, return on assets is calculated by dividing a company's net earnings by its total assets. The higher the return, the more efficient management is in utilizing its asset base. For instance, ROA ratio for notable, established companies like General Electric and Microsoft are 2.3% and 18.0% respectively. However, a growth penny stock may have a considerably smaller figure.

## ROE

ROE or "return on net worth" is calculated by taking the net income and dividing it by the total shareholders' equity. This will show how effectively a company generates a return on the capital provided by investors. If the company retains these profits, the common shareholders will only realize this gain by having an appreciated stock.

Best way to track a company's progress and earnings, is to calculate ROE and ROA at the beginning of a period and at the end of a period to see the change in return. There is hardly a magic number you should be looking for here. Instead, compare these numbers to industry averages, and you'll get an idea where this company stands among its competitors.

## Competitive Advantage

Comparing the metrics above with other companies is one way to discover a company's competitive advantage. Other ways to garner this important quality include comparing ability to keep costs low in production, brand recognition, even the date the company started, etc.

**Brand Recognition**

However, there are other factors that aren't as measurable. A big one is brand recognition, which is the extent to which a consumer can correctly identify a particular product only by its logo, tag line, packaging, etc. For instance, Canopy Growth Corp. has 'WEED' as its ticker symbol on the Toronto Stock Exchange. This is great branding, since a ticker symbol like this can easily get the attention of investors looking to get in the "weed game".

**Location**

Another competitive advantage could be the location of a company's facilities or operations. In regards to producing marijuana, it's much more advantageous to be a company based near states where cannabis is legal, as opposed to states that aren't. For instance, Terra Tech Corporation has a competitive advantage, since its operations are based near most of the states that recently voted for recreational marijuana legalization.

**Partnerships and Contracts**

Partnerships and contracts, especially with big companies, offer a big competitive advantage as well. As mentioned in the last chapter, AusCann's share price has done so well partly because of its affiliations with major companies in Canada and Brazil. Same can be said for Canopy Growth's operations in Germany, or Medical Marijuana Inc's partnerships with Mexico.

In addition, contracts with celebrities can be huge for brand recognition. Canopy Growth Corp. jumped to record high prices after unveiling a line of marijuana products for the domestic market in a partnership with rapper, Snoop Dogg.

## Analyst Coverage and Conference Calls

While plenty of analyst coverage is bogus, it is still a good policy to pay attention. It will often impact a stock. Though most qualified analysts will not cover penny stocks, they will often cover marijuana penny stocks because of how hot they are. The winners and losers in this industry can be made or broken based on analysts coverage. Articles on breakthrough contract wins or earnings reports are often big news. If an analyst does write an article, pay attention how it affects the company in question.

Same goes for conference calls. Companies will usually announce them anywhere from the day before to a few weeks ahead of time. Positive conference calls can really separate the winners from the losers, so pay attention.

# SEC Suspensions or Halts

When following companies, you may hear of SEC trading suspensions or halts. With penny stocks especially, these things happen, usually after big pump and dump-induced runups or other forms of manipulation. SEC (The Securities and Exchange Commission) is a government commission created by the United States Congress with goals of protecting investors, maintaining fair and orderly functioning of securities markets, and facilitating capital formation.

Many penny stocks, including many marijuana stocks, don't file with the SEC. If you're investing in a company's stock that doesn't file with the SEC, it's better to dump them. There's probably a good reason they aren't reporting and it's simply not worth it to you to hold onto their shares. A lot of manipulation happens in the stock market, but especially with penny stocks in a burgeoning industry like this one with many competitors. Investors can reference the SEC's EDGAR database to see if a company files with the SEC.

By checking SEC filings, investors can verify information they've heard about the company. Also, these filings can offer a hidden store of insight, but that insight only matters if it's been independently audited by accountants. For instance, if looking at filings, you notice the company has changed its name four times in five years, that's a red flag signaling a potentially terrible trade.

## Lawsuits

Investors should also investigate company's lawsuits. A company being sued is not a reason for panic and to close all your shares. But why is it being sued? If a company made a mistake and is immediately rectifying the situation, it still may be worth holding onto the stock, especially if your investment was made for the long term. After all, a few of the leading licensed producers in the Canadian exchange have already been sued, such as Canopy Growth Corp. and Organigram. It's sometimes just the price of business.

Nevertheless, it is a wise policy to pay attention. Sometimes a company is sued for reasons that reveal the company's illegitimacy. Either way, lawsuits will often greatly affect the share price.

## In Conclusion

To find the most promising companies in this heap of promising companies, investors need to look hard into every aspect of a company and its coverage by the media. Investors should analyze a variety of angles that provide glimpses into its efficiency, plans for the future, profitability, industry reputation, competitive advantages and disadvantages.

Finally, never forget that the cannabis industry is still growing in conjunction with regulations and an always-evolving legislation throughout the world. Deviations are to be expected. As is true throughout the markets, nothing is a forgone conclusion. Even thoughtful investing in this burgeoning market can be riskier than usual, but it's also incredibly exciting and potentially hugely rewarding.

# Stock Trading Strategies

As mentioned earlier, this book assumes you have experience as a stock trader. It will not be going into detail about stock terms, such as short selling, limit prices and stop losses. Nor will the book get into the details of studying charts when conducting technical analysis. You're going to have to learn about those elsewhere. While these can be simple terms by definition, they can be very complicated and go beyond the scope of this book. However, there's mountains of information on how to use them online. Instead, this chapter will focus on general trading concepts to use for the kind of growth stocks covered in this book.

Just a reminder, any industry still in its infancy has many risks in regards to investing. As an example, just study the dot com bubble that bursts in the early 2000's. The risk associated with trading marijuana stocks means that they might be best suited for the more aggressive, seasoned investor. If you are a more conservative trader, it may be worth it to you to wait and see how the industry plays out in several years, though you will indeed miss its largest profits.

# Designing Your Strategy

Your stock trading strategy should obviously be designed so that you can trade successfully. Your strategy should allow you to enter and exit trades in anticipation of price changes in the market.

Compare stock trading to playing chess, in that successful chess players design strategies specific to the types of opponents they may face. They anticipate their opponent's moves based upon their chosen strategy. And they play offense and defense. As a trader you must not only use defensive moves to protect your capital, but use offensive moves in order to grow capital through profitable trades.

When you design a strategy, important factors to consider include:

- Type of Trader You Are

- The Amount of Available Capital

- When to Enter and Exit Trades

# Type of Trader You Are

What kind of trader you are largely depends on your risk tolerance. If you are more risk averse, a buy and hold strategy with companies you like is your best bet.

## Buy and Hold Strategy

The buy-and-hold strategy ignores short term movements of share price. Instead, the investor concentrates on the long term. He or she believes that price movements over the long term will outweigh the price movements in the short term.

## Active Trading Strategy

Active traders, however, believe that short-term volatility of share prices are where the profits are made. There are various ways to accomplish an active-trading strategy. Besides the VERY active trading strategies known as 'Day Trading' and 'Scalping', there are two other types of active trading that are not quite as dependent on volatility and therefore, better suited for the long term success of this sector.

## 1. Position Trading

Position traders (or Trend traders) look to determine the direction of the market, but they do not try to forecast any price action. Typically, trend traders jump on the trend after it has established itself, and when the trend breaks, they usually close their position. Position trading requires that investors discover the trend through fundamental analysis (news) and/ or technical analysis (charts). In essence, trend traders look for successive higher highs or lower highs in price action to determine the trend of a stock.

For instance, when Trump's administration told the press they would likely be taking action against the states that had legalized recreational marijuana, it put all marijuana stocks on a temporary downtrend-- even pot stocks on foreign exchanges. If you are a position trader, this would have been a time to lessen your positions until the trend ended.

## 2. Swing Trading

On the other hand, swing traders enter at the end of trends. How? Well there is often volatility at the end of a trend when it's about to reverse itself. In addition, the news can create new trends-- such as earnings reports or conference calls. For instance, when Canada begins to implement its cannabis legalization through a set of laws in 2018, it will likely create an uptrend. At this time, an investor would add to those positions.

# The Amount of Available Capital

An investor should never trade without adequate capital. Just like the companies you're trading, not having enough capital in relation to the trades you make can often lead to trouble. It's poor risk and money management.

The amount of working capital that you will need depends on a number of factors. Some of those factors include: Capital Requirement for Diversification, Capital Requirement for Dollar Cost Averaging, Your Trading Goals and Margin Requirements.

## Capital Requirement for Diversification

For instance, if you want to invest $10,000 in one stock, but have $15,000 total opening account balance, that will leave you only $5,000 to invest in other stocks. This would be very poor diversification. Therefore, in order to diversify your portfolio more evenly and yet still hold a $10k position in that first stock, it's probably better to have a lot more capital-- say at least $100k available.

## Capital Requirement for Dollar Cost Averaging

Dollar-cost averaging is an investment technique of buying a fixed amount of shares on a regular schedule, regardless of its price. The investor may buy more shares when the price is low and fewer shares when the price is high.

In the same example above, suppose your stock goes down in value by 5%, but you believe this is just a temporary correction and not a continuous downtrend. You may decide you would like to add to your position to reap the net profit from the retracement. However, if you don't have enough capital, then you cannot buy these discounted shares. Many investors do this 'dollar cost averaging' periodically. If this is your strategy as well, adequate capital is necessary to reap the benefits.

## Your Trading Goals

Your trading goals are an important factor in determining your capital requirement as well. For instance, if you are looking to create $100,000 per year in income through trading, this will require $1 Million if you are fortunate enough to create a 10% yield off your portfolio.

## Margin Requirements

Margin trading allows you to leverage the assets in your account (cash and securities) to purchase more securities than you would be able to buy on a cash-only basis. You are trading with borrowed funds. Therefore, there is a potential for increased gains as well as increased losses.

If you decide the risk of margin loans is right for you, they can be a low-cost, flexible way to borrow funds for your trading strategy. This is especially true if you use a brokerage like Interactive Brokers which charges around 2.5% interest-- or less depending on the amount of capital you have. That sounds more cost effective than credit cards and most other types of lending.

Margin loans aren't for everyone. It presents many unique risks, with the biggest being losing more capital than your original investment. However, if you improve your money and risk management skills, margins can be used to increase your market exposure by providing fast access to cash at opportune times.

## Margin Maintenance & Risks

Each broker requires an initial deposit to request margin privileges. For instance, Scottrade requires a low $2,000. Once a loan is extended, you're required to keep a minimum equity level. This is called the maintenance requirement.

The two biggest risks of margin trading are amplified losses and margin calls. Due to increased market exposure, it's possible to lose more funds than the initial capital deposited in your account. If that occurs, you won't just be responsible for paying back the loan. You will also have to pay the interest. Keep in mind interest rates may fluctuate during the time your loan is outstanding.

All brokers require you to keep a minimum equity level in your account at all times. If you fall below this minimum maintenance requirement, your broker may issue a margin call that requires you to deposit cash or close trades immediately. If you're unable to do either of these things, your broker may need to force the closing of some or all of your securities to bring your account back below the equity requirement.

# When to Enter and Exit Trades

When deciding on when to enter a trade, it is important for an investor to get rid of all the noise and focus. Only then will an investor understand the prevailing trend and capitalize on it. While this book promotes investing in marijuana stocks for the long term, it is still important to familiarize yourself with the current trends so that you will maximize your profits. This is especially true considering all the volatility this sector has had and will have in the future.

Below is a list of general rules to entering and exiting trades that will help you find the greatest potential for profit with the lowest risk. There is always risks with trading in a burgeoning industry, but by sticking to these rules the chances of making successful trades suddenly turn in your favor. These rules take advantage of the fact that the market ebbs and flows in waves. Much of it is common sense, but beginning traders often do not listen to common sense and instead let their emotions dictate their choices.

**1. When marijuana stocks are uptrending, buy the stronger companies. When marijuana stocks are downtrending, sell the weaker companies.**

Why?

When the there is a pullback, a stronger stock's share price will not go down as much-- if at all. These are the same stocks to trade in an uptrend. Companies like Aphria Inc.

and Canopy Growth Corp. are the current leaders of this sector and they are the ones that move the market higher, with minimal pullbacks.

For instance, when Trump's administration insinuated that they would take action against states that legalized recreational marijuana, cannabis stocks around the world deflated in share price. But Canadian Aphria Inc. barely moved compared to the rest. Why? This is likely due to investors knowing Aphria was one of the few cannabis companies that has continuous positive cash flow despite huge expansion projects. This is no small feat.

By the same token, an investor should short sell the weaker penny stocks when the marijuana stock market is downtrending. Short sell these stocks because they will likely drop in price more than the market. At the time of this writing, there is at least a few hundred marijuana stocks trading on markets around the world. Some of the stronger stocks of that bunch have been listed In this book. Therefore, there is plenty of riskier, smaller stocks out there perfect for short selling.

This strategy should provide more safety and relative outperformance profits. Keep in mind, since the list of relatively strong stocks and the list of relatively weak stocks can change periodically, it becomes necessary to study the companies in question using the principles touched upon in the last chapter.

## 2. Wait for the Pullback

With nearly all trends-- up or down, there are always pullbacks in the share price as day traders collect small profits. The market moves in waves for this reason, sometimes mysteriously. When studying an uptrending line on a chart, you may notice almost a staircase pattern, or in other words, higher highs and lower lows.

Therefore, it's often good practice to enter a long position after the price moves down toward the trendline and then moves back higher. In simplistic terms, buy at the beginning of the next upward wave to obtain more profits. Or if you are short selling, wait until the price moves up the downward sloping trendline and make your entry when the stock begins to move back down.

It is important for an investor to be patient with this type of strategy. However, a noticeable pullback may not come if a surging stock is hot enough. This is where your due diligence is required. If your research shows this trend is not slowing down, you may have to start a position as soon as you can. Researching the company with the principles outlined in the previous chapter will help an investor discern between a trend based on hype or a trend based on valid fundamentals.

Sometimes a pullback is more than just a pullback. It could be the start of a downward trend. Again, due diligence is required. It's usually wise practice to not add to a losing stock. However, its sudden spiral downward could be due to a correction in the whole sector and not because of anything wrong with the company. If this is the case, you will have more opportunities to obtain shares of the stock at discounted prices. This is why it is important to practice money management. In other words, do not use up all your capital every time you add to a position. If you do, you may not have enough to add to future positions when there are future pullbacks- big or small. Instead, add to your position with small doses of capital-- only if you believe a retracement will happen. This will result in an overall net profit.

## 3. Profit Taking

Unless your strategy is buy and hold, usually you will want to close a position before a correction occurs. Since markets move in waves in all time periods, it should be evident what a stock's previous highs and lows are. These are often used for reference when determining entry and exit points.

Therefore, the strategy with the lowest risk is this: if you have a long position and your stock is in an uptrend, take profits at the former price high. If you have a short position and your stock is in a downtrend, take profits at the former price low.

## 4. Buy at the Breakout

Keep in mind, the stocks in question in this book are growth stocks. Therefore, it is very likely these stocks could explode past their previous price highs. When a stock surges past its resistance point (prior price high) without slowing down, that is a pretty good indication it is on its way to a longer trend. Do your due diligence-- Find out why it's surging. If its fundamentals are relatively sound, you probably want to enter a position to see what new highs this stock might take you.

## 5. When low risk entries are not visible, step aside.

Traders should generally trade with the overall trend and patiently wait for low risk entries to make the odds of obtaining profit more likely. However, sometimes the signals to buy or sell are not obvious. If this is the case, you don't have to do anything. It's better to just step aside and wait for a more visible signal. Funny enough, this is often the most difficult thing for most investors to do. They often get too emotional. They feel the need to do something, which results in making bad decisions.

## Conclusion- Cut Losses / Let Profits Run!

There is no such thing as a perfect strategy. Sometimes, a trading strategy will not be in tune with current market sentiment despite your carefully planned research. Consequently, your strategy may result in a string of consecutive losing trades. During these times, it is important you preserve working capital.

By managing your risk properly and preserving working capital, you can weather-these-storms. Proper risk management will control your losses in such a way to keep them manageable and not catastrophic. A catastrophic loss means you can't even continue to trade and recoup your losses. Don't let this happen to you!

In most trading strategies, the objective is not having the highest possible percentage of winning trades, but instead to trade profitably over a long term. In fact, some investors are quite profitable only winning 50% of their trades. Or even less. How? They cut their losses quickly, but they let their profits run as high as they may go. What really matters in the long run is that the sum total of profits is greater than the sum total of losses.

# Sources

All of the factual information in this book, including stock statistics and government legislation, was compiled from a myriad of sources, including news media websites and websites compiling data for research. Below is a list that includes these sources.

It is recommended that readers of this book visit these websites, since stocks and government legislation could change from one moment to the next. To deepen your research further, use Google Alerts to monitor the web for up to the minute news on anything related to marijuana. To create a list of alerts, visit Google Alerts and in the box at the top, enter a topic you want to follow. Google will then send you an email when there are new results for your topic. These emails will arrive in your inbox as often as you like, and the topics you entered can be changed at any time.

www.seekingalpha.com - A crowd-sourced content service for financial markets, including stock market Insights & financial analysis, free earnings call transcripts, investment ideas and ETF & stock research, all written by finance experts.

www.bloomberg.com - Bloomberg delivers business and markets news, data, analysis, and video to the world, featuring stories from Businessweek and Bloomberg News.

www.investorplace.com - InvestorPlace provides millions of investors with insightful articles, free stock picks and stock market news.

www.investopedia.com - "Investopedia is the world's leading source of financial content on the web, ranging from market news to retirement strategies, investing education to insights from around the world."

www.thecannabist.co - Marijuana news and culture, research, resources, strain reviews, cannabutter recipes, vaporizer & cannabis concentrates info, hemp, Colorado dispensary map.

www.bezinga.com - Stock Market Quotes, Business News, Financial News, Trading Ideas, and Stock Research by Professionals.

www.theguardian.com - Billing itself as the world's leading liberal voice, the Guardian is a British daily newspaper with the latest world news, sports, business, opinion, analysis and reviews.

www.leafly.com - Leafly provides visitors with reviews of the best medical cannabis strains.

"Leafly is the largest cannabis website in the world, with over 10 million monthly visitors and 40 million page views across its website and mobile applications." - Wikipedia.org

www.cnn.com - View the latest news and breaking news today for U.S., world, weather, entertainment, politics and health at CNN.com.

"The Cable News Network is an American basic cable and satellite television news channel owned by the Turner Broadcasting System division of Time Warner. It was founded in 1980 by American media proprietor Ted Turner as a 24-hour cable news channel." - Wikipedia.org

www.naturalnews.com - Independent News on Natural Health and the World. Natural News is a science-based natural health advocacy organization led by activist-turned-scientist Mike Adams, the Health Ranger.

www.marijuanastocks.com - "Our goal is to become the central hub for all who are seeking current Marijuana Stock News as well as cannabis industry, political and social news, articles, trends & overall insight, delivered in a way that we all can relate to."

www.cnbc.com - Latest business news on stock markets, financial & earnings. View world markets streaming charts & video; check stock tickers and quotes.

www.fool.com - The Motley Fool is a multimedia financial-services company that provides leading insight and analysis about stocks, investing, and personal finance services.

www.newcannabisventures.com - Contributing original content and curating quality news on only the most promising cannabis companies and the most influential investors, allowing you to save time as you stay on top of the latest trends in this dynamic industry.

www.insiderfinancial.com - Insider Financial offers stock news & analysis on U.S. equities.

www.streetregister.com – Wall Street Financial News and Analyst Insights.

"Our mission is to provide unmatched news and insight on newsworthy and momentum stocks for traders and investors. At Street Register we believe that there are plenty of emerging growth companies across a variety of industry sectors with plenty of hidden value. Market discovery and innovation often occurs in small to mid-size companies that are either misunderstood or underrepresented. We focus on identifying these companies and uncovering their stories before the rest of the market to ensure that you receive the full story – every single day."

www.nytimes.com - Breaking news, multimedia, reviews & opinion on Washington, business, sports, movies, travel, books, jobs, education, real estate and financial markets.

www.forbes.com - Forbes is an American business magazine focused on original articles about business, investing, technology, entrepreneurship, leadership, and lifestyle.

www.merryjane.com - "Merry Jane is the definitive cannabis resource offering exclusive content and relatable perspectives on culture, news, video, food, and style."

www.nasdaq.com - Named after the second-largest exchange in the world by market capitalization, the Nasdaq Stock Market website features stock quotes and analysis.


www.newswire.ca - Cited as the most-referenced source of Canadian news releases for journalists, Canada Newswire engages with audiences across the globe.

# Conclusion

We certainly hope you enjoyed reading "International Marijuana" as much as we enjoyed writing it. The effort and opportunity in researching and writing this book has been an enriching experience for everyone involved. Not to mention, it even deepened our own understanding of the industry and made our own investment choices even clearer.

Remember, as with most books about stocks, some of the material will become dated with time. This is why we also included chapters meant to teach investors how to research companies as fundamentals and the industry changes.

Finally, if you enjoyed this book, please take the time to share your thoughts and post a review. It would be greatly appreciated.

Made in the USA
Middletown, DE
24 January 2019